WORKING TOWARDS BALANCE

Our Society in the
New Millennium

Edited by Harry Bohan and Gerard Kennedy

VERITAS

First published 2000 by
Veritas Publications
7/8 Lower Abbey Street
Dublin 1

ISBN 1 85390 474 0

British Library Cataloguing
in Publication Data.
A catalogue record for
this book is available
from the British Library.

Grateful acknowledgement is made to Salmon Publishing Ltd, Galway, for permission to reproduce 'The Betrayal' by Michael D. Higgins

Cover design by Barbara Croatto, with graphics by Avid Design, Limerick
Printed in the Republic of Ireland by Betaprint Ltd, Dublin

Looking at the title that Fr Harry Bohan and his team chose for this conference it is obvious that they have touched on a subject that was in danger of being subsumed by a fast-changing society.

The 'Working Towards Balance' conference has facilitated a meeting of minds, a meeting of concepts and ideas and I am in no doubt that many issues will be more effectively addressed as a result of the commitment of those who attended and participated in this conference.

Barney Whelan
Manager, Public Relations,
Conference Sponsor ESB

CONTENTS

FOREWORD

Harry Bohan

Our economy is booming and Irish society is undergoing extraordinary transformations. The economic boom is driven by technology – for the most part overseas-sourced technology and finance. As this new Ireland is being let loose, the old one is losing much of its shine. The first victims of the new openness were the great institutions of Church and State. We are now facing profound social and moral issues that need to be identified, researched and debated. That is why our conferences and our recently established Applied Research Centre are attracting such interest.

In November 1998, our organisation, Rural Resource Development Ltd, ran a conference in Ennis titled 'Are We Forgetting Something? – Our Society in the New Millennium'. It turned out to be, as Marie Martin from Omagh, one of the chairpeople, put it, 'like no other' in many ways. The first day, she said, 'brought together some of the finest speakers it has ever been my privilege to hear, and raised very high expectations – which were subsequently fulfilled – for the second and third day'. The 'Are We Forgetting Something?' Conference proved to be an unforgettable experience. There was so much to absorb from those amazing days. Crucial issues focusing on the direction that Irish society is taking were discussed and debated. An average of four hundred people per day, representing a cross-section of Irish society, took part – approximately one thousand people in all touched in. The published papers of that conference, also titled *Are We Forgetting Something?*, have been equally successful and have given thousands more the opportunity to link into some provocative, incisive and visionary thoughts.

The big message from that conference was that technology has transformed the nature of Irish society and its effect is multiplied by the fact that the economy – and therefore the society – is driven by investment from global technology companies. Science has produced the technology that underpins everything, from our economy to our health and lifestyles. It dominates our daily lives by its amazingly successful applications. We are now very much part of the global society. However, when a society decides to fly on one wing, the fall-out can be serious, particularly in the area of relationships. These can be categorised into four areas:

- inner-self – undernourished spirit, soul.
- others – what is happening to family, community.
- creation – uprootedness leading to waywardness, loss of a sense of place, fears, aloneness, disconnecting from nature, wastage of natural resources.
- creator – God becomes less and we become great.

So, it would appear that there is a two-way pull on our minds and hearts – by globalisation on the one hand, and by the need for meaning and direction – 'where people are' – on the other. There is no denying which is in the ascendancy and so there is a need to restore the balance.

We were determined that, because the conference touched on some issues that were to the forefront in people's minds, we would follow up with action. Issues raised included the relationship of corporations to families and communities, the force of voluntarism, local resources, the social economy and spiritual needs and values.

An Applied Research Centre was established, with the emphasis on 'applied'. Academics, business people, people from the worlds of law, education, medicine, visionaries and practitioners have come together with us to identify through research the direction that Ireland is taking. Voluntarism provides many of the services that people require. There is a great spiritual energy generated in a people caring for one another. A network of voluntary organisations has been established and is beginning to function very effectively.

Working Towards Balance
This brings us to our second conference. The theme 'Working Towards Balance' is a follow-on from one of the most powerful messages of the previous year. The conference participants represented a wide spectrum of Irish society.

The speakers were Fintan O'Toole (Does Power Erode Ethics?), Catherine McGeachy (The Human Dimension in the Workplace), Stephen Covey (Corporate Responsibility to Communities), Tom Collins (Ireland: The Challenges of Success), Miriam Moore (Love and Work in the Millennium: A Vision for Personal Balance and Development), Richard Douthwaite (The Growth Illusion) and John O'Donohue (Is Balance a Myth? Creativity Awakens Only at the Edge). Harry Bohan gave an update on the Applied Research Centre, which was founded last year, and Mary Redmond gave an update on 'The Wheel', a network of voluntary groups, the seeds for which were sown at last year's conference. Sessions were chaired by Ciaran Lynch, Kevin Kelly, John Cushnahan and Marian Harkin. The Electricity Supply Board was our sponsor. There was almost unanimous agreement that this was a superb conference. Many of the participants responded to our invitation to let us know in writing 'what they heard'. We are following this up with the invitation to participants to let us know what action they have taken within their spheres of influence.

This conference underlined the importance of restoring the balance between ideology and technology, between the demands of family life and the demands of the workplace, between powerlessness and an ethics system that is rooted in people being given and taking responsibility. We are a society in transition. We have moved from the authoritarianism of the Church to the authoritarianism of the box in the corner and the computer. The clericalised Church was an overlord. The religious process was one of compliance. To search or explore was almost treasonable. Religious maturity was confused with ritualistic compliance. Powerlessness, fear and lack of confidence in ourselves as a people were some of the results.

We are now in the process of moving out of this kind of authoritarianism, but what are we moving towards? We need to debate issues that are fundamental to any stable society. Our economic success is welcome. We are now in a position to make choices. The fundamental weakness of the ethics system of the past was that it came from the top down – it wasn't about people making choices. As that kind of coercive society began to disappear, as the old system unravelled, we moved into a free-for-all. We then saw massive indulgence in unethical behaviour. The key period in the shaping of modern Ireland was the late eighties and early nineties. We had lost the restraints for people in power without having anything to replace them.

Now in a period dominated by technology, we wonder who is rearing the next generation. For example, parents spend 40 per cent less time with their children than they did twenty years ago. There is a war going on for the hearts and minds of young people. So, we are very exposed as we move into the new millennium. We are going into it at a time when consumerism gives us our identity. The cult of consumerism is dominant.

The major challenge now facing Irish society is to develop a partnership to promote values – individual, family and community values. In the past, the Church had almost a copyright on values. Now we are very much influenced by corporate values. Corporations can no longer ignore the environment in which they operate. If the organisations of work and the consumer society undermine relationships within families and between neighbours, then isolationism and loneliness will take their toll and our economic success will be short-lived. People thrive in an atmosphere of trust and of community. There is evidence to suggest that the spiritual healing and counselling industries are thriving. This suggests that another form of powerlessness dominates. Cynicism is a symptom of a deep, chronic problem.

And so we face the challenge of restoring the balance. If, in the past, we had the ethic of powerlessness, now we must move to the ethic of power. We must empower the people and this must begin with respect. This must be a process that brings together spirituality and politics, spirituality and work, infusing a spiritual grace that belongs to all of us in the public and private spheres. The new ethic, the new morality must begin by returning to the people at all levels. Change is staggering. A mature leadership at all levels is called for so that each individual takes responsibility for his or her sphere of *influence* rather than his or her sphere of *concern.*

The issues raised at this conference call for the creation of a new moral and social order. This must emerge from a partnership with the focus on people and where they are. Although painful at times, these issues need to be debated. In our search for the truth, we demonstrate a maturity that demands that we be brutally honest. Being honest in this way may well lead to a type of spirituality that takes account of who we are, where we have come from and, more importantly, where we are going. The conference is a call to examine the rapid changes taking place in our society. It is the responsibility of the individual to guide and direct these changes. In doing so we can live, love and work in a society that strives to leave a legacy for future generations.

What is Happening to Family?

Despite all the massive changes that are taking place in Ireland, the real struggle in our society at this time is not with the institutions of Church and State, but with the relentless transfer of power from the family to the anonymous and institutional. This change has been taking place in Ireland for the past thirty years and it continues to intensify with every year that passes. The recent Budget emphasised the fact that the family must now satisfy the insatiable hunger of the labour market. Herein lies a major contradiction. The Constitution of Ireland has this to say about the family in Article 41:

> The State recognises the family as the natural primary and fundamental unit group of society. . . . The State, therefore, guarantees to protect the family in its constitution and authority, as the necessary basis of social order and as indispensable to the welfare of the Nation and the State.

Leaders – Church and State – agree that there is nothing that can take the place of the family. No amount of helping services can make up for its failures; no welfare agency works nearly as well. Over the centuries, the family has ensured the health and stability of Irish society. I don't think many would deny that nothing can take the place of the family. However, the typical family unit in modern society is probably more isolated and vulnerable than ever before, and herein lies the contradiction. To my limited knowledge of human history, it is not until we come to modern society that we find the isolated nuclear family as it exists today, often removed from the extended family, and sometimes isolated even from the local community. If this is the reality, then what we describe as 'the fundamental unit group of society' is virtually unable on its own to sustain any one of the functions it undertook up to modern times.

For example, responsibility for education and preparation for life is passed on in turn to pre-school, school and university, with the support of educational authorities and the Department of Education. Responsibility for maintenance of basic health is passed on to the crowded doctor's office, the impersonal outpatient clinic and sterile hospital ward, backed by Health Boards, professional medical and nursing organisations and the Department of Health. Responsibility for the provision of food and the necessities of life is passed on to mechanised agricultural and manufacturing industries and distributed through massive supermarkets. The scale of rules and regulations that are imposed by bureaucracies of one kind or another on house construction and purchase is enormous. The family could be dealing with three solicitors and a number of financial institutions when buying a house.

The teaching of religion, for the most part, has been passed on to the Church and there is a strong possibility now that the family is generally unprepared to pass on the faith to its children. Some parents may remain at a level of pious belonging to the Church without having educated themselves in religious doctrines and beliefs. Many parents would seem to have an undernourished faith that may well suffice for them, but, in a very real way, that undernourishment may be passed on to their children.

As this process of transfer of responsibility for basic functions, from the personal to the bureaucratic, continues, we begin to hear of the problems. We hear of the geriatric problem, the problems of adolescence, and the problems of childcare. We are witnessing the segregation of the elderly into institutions or ghettos through the movement of young married families to suburban housing estates. This same movement is a major factor in the creation of the isolated nuclear family, bringing in its wake many of the tensions that are pressurising families today.

What does all this do to the family? What is it doing to our elderly, to our young? Of course, it can be argued that the family has no choice but to hand over responsibility to impersonal organisations. No one, however, has as yet claimed to have found a satisfactory substitute for carrying out the intimate and subtle tasks traditionally assumed by the various generations of a family. Nor can these be handed over to anyone else. The loving relationship between man and woman is the vital factor from which all else in marriage and family life follows. If there is an over-reliance on the emotional, then the relationship in marriage becomes very fragile, and there is certainly no substitute for a positive, loving relationship when it comes to rearing children.

The Irish family, which has undergone a major transformation in the past generation, is poised to change even more in the coming decades. Both family values and family structure have been changing and, as a result, the Irish family is a much-changed institution. Work has become central to both partners in marriage. We continue to aspire to traditional values regarding the importance of marriage and family, but we have organised society in such a way that relationships have become almost commercialised.

The real challenge for our society in the future will be to return to the family and the community. We cannot continue to allow big organisations of any kind to disempower people in their basic units of society. We need a new social and moral order within which people are at the centre and organisations and institutions facilitate. That is the task being undertaken by our newly established centre. Connecting with one another in family and community will be the focus of this work.

Thanks

We wish to thank Máire Johnston, conference co-ordinator, Rural Resource Development Ltd staff, the conference committee and the volunteers who gave so generously of their time. We are deeply indebted to the speakers and chairpeople for their valuable contributions and their enthusiasm. We would like to thank the West County Hotel, Ennis Information Age Town for kindly sponsoring Dr Stephen Covey's video link, and especially our overall sponsor, the ESB. We are also grateful for the considerable coverage of the event as well as the promotional work done on behalf of the conference by James Morrissey.

SUMMARY OF OPENING ADDRESS

GER LOUGHNANE AND SEAN BOYLAN

Management and Motivation

The opening address was given by two of the most successful sports managers in Ireland in recent times. Sean Boylan, the longest-serving Gaelic football manager in Ireland, has guided Meath to five All-Ireland titles, the most recent in 1999, while Ger Loughnane has taken Clare to the Promised Land, winning three Munster hurling titles and two All-Irelands during the nineties. Collectively they know more than most on the theme of 'Management and Motivation', the subject of the opening address.

On the subject of team management, Sean Boylan refers to the responsibility that the manager holds. He believes that the need to respect and value the individuals involved is very important. 'All we have to try and do, as best we can, is create the right environment, and don't abuse the privilege that we have, because it is a huge responsibility,' says Sean. Bringing out the leadership skills among team members is a key issue for Ger Loughnane. 'As a manager, your job is to get them to be the leaders. In any organisation you must have leaders,' he says. Sean agrees: 'Our job is not to put down players but rather to encourage, to help lads to face up to things and confront problems.' 'You love to see a team playing with the same drive and passion as you have yourself,' says Ger. 'You must keep control in a really tense situation and stick to the game plan and remind people what their responsibility is,' he adds.

Maintaining a sense of humour is something that Sean Boylan believes is crucial in assisting team spirit while Ger is a great believer in putting things into perspective. Acknowledging that the greatest lesson he has taken from his long-time involvement in sport is the importance of home and family and the support that this offers, he quotes from the great US swimmer Matt Biandi, about dealing with disappointment: 'I thought I was going to win, but when all is said and done and when I go home, my dog will still lick my face.'

While both men are passionate about sport they also believe that involvement in sport and the thin line between victory and defeat ensure that all good managers are very aware of the need to achieve balance. According to Sean Boylan, 'Balance is crucial. You can be passionate about something, but it's important that you don't become fanatical about it. If you do you'll miss all of the simple things that are around you. Sport is a huge part of my life, but I like music, I like reading, and I love people and that's the thing that gives me the balance. I'm lucky to be involved with the soil and the earth as well, and somehow that balances me.'

'It's so easy in modern life, with its pace and everything else, to get carried away with one aspect of your life,' agrees Ger Loughnane. 'People who are involved in sport are generally balanced people. Sport keeps that balance.' He believes that 'When you are in charge of a team, keeping the balance is absolutely vital.' Ger's philosophy is that 'Balance leads to happiness. Balance is the secret to happiness in life. We can never achieve it completely, but we can always aim towards it. The nearer we get to achieving it, the happier we are.'

1

DOES POWER ERODE ETHICS?

FINTAN O'TOOLE

It is a genuine privilege and pleasure to be here right now. I think we are all very conscious in our daily lives that we are living at a time of dizzying and sometimes bewildering change and that the nature of what is around us has become increasingly unpredictable and unfamiliar. As someone who is at the moment moving back and forth between New York and Dublin quite frequently, it does sometimes strike me that contemporary Ireland can at times seem as strange as Manhattan. It seems as much 'abroad' for those of us who grew up in the Ireland of the 1960s as places that we're used to thinking of as exotic and far away. A lot of us feel like the familiar caricature of the returned Yank in Irish folklore, drama and fiction. Even if we have never left, many of us find ourselves going around like returned Yanks asking, 'What used to be there?' and, 'Gee, is that building gone?'

In this kind of atmosphere it is crucial for us, right now, to have moments of punctuation like this, where we try to reflect on who we are and where we are, and where we might possibly be going. I think it is immensely important that this is being done and for that reason it is a great privilege to be invited to be part of it.

One of the great clichés when anybody talks about power and ethics is the well-known phrase that power corrupts, and absolute power corrupts absolutely. I don't think anybody at the end of the twentieth century would seriously doubt that this is one of those statements that has become a cliché, because it is so obviously true. We know, through the terrible history of the century, that people who are given untrammelled power, power without accountability, will abuse it. That follows, almost as night follows day. It is a terrible reflection, but one that is very difficult to avoid for anybody who looks back over the past hundred years or even over the past fifty years.

But I would like to start by suggesting that, while it is undoubtedly true that absolute power corrupts absolutely, we could also reverse that statement and it would be equally true. We could also say that powerlessness corrupts and that absolute powerlessness corrupts absolutely. I think it is in the intersection between those contrary statements that we find ourselves as a society at the moment. I would like to reflect on this for a little while. The idea that powerlessness corrupts is somewhat less familiar than the idea that power without accountability will be abused, but it is equally fundamental to any reflection on the nature of society and particularly on the nature of contemporary Ireland. Morality is based on one very fundamental human quality, which is the quality of choice. If you don't have a choice about how you act, then you cannot act morally. If you don't have decisions to make, you cannot make ethical decisions. The state of being without the capacity to make choices or decisions is powerlessness.

Most of us who pay PAYE taxes, for instance, can look back and say, well, we have been more moral or more ethical than those who did not pay PAYE taxes, because we paid our taxes and they didn't. That is perhaps quite a comforting notion. But on the other hand, we also have to question whether we had any choice in the matter. Our state of being morally justified is somewhat undermined by the fact that most of us were not in a position to do otherwise. If we had been in a position to do otherwise, perhaps we might have done otherwise.

That is a simple illustration of what I am trying to get at, which is that morality or ethical behaviour is fundamentally rooted in a certain kind of freedom; in the ability to do otherwise, to be elsewhere, to take other kinds of directions. And it is that openness of choice that is lacking in the condition of powerlessness. The condition of powerlessness, I think, is one that in many ways characterises much of what Irish society has been through until the very recent past. If we did act morally, it was, paradoxically, because we didn't have the freedom to do otherwise.

Powerlessness corrupts by eroding the sense of personal responsibility that is central to any kind of ethical conduct. It does not just stop at the fact that you don't in a specific case have a choice to make. It also creates a culture in which, through not exercising choices, you lose the capacity to choose. You lose the capacity to take responsibility for your actions.

Again, I think most of us have a sense of this. Take, for example, court cases where somebody goes in and says, 'Yes, I murdered my mother, but I did it because of society. I did it because of the terrible things that were done to me'. Most of us know that this kind of plea is both true and untrue. It is an excuse, an escape from responsibility. But it is also rooted in a reality; people who don't have any kind of power don't develop a sense of responsibility and don't develop a capacity to feel responsible for their own actions. That, too, is a kind of corruption.

This strange sense in which both power and powerlessness can corrupt is something that leads to some of the more difficult and unpleasant aspects of human history. One of the phenomena that we have had to face in the twentieth century, for instance, is the fact that very frequently a kind of collusion develops between victims and their oppressors. So that the corruption of absolute power and the corruption of absolute powerlessness become part of the same thing. We know from studies of concentration camps, for example, that in the most horrible and extreme of human circumstances some people will adapt to survival by colluding with the people who are running the camps, by attempting to identify more with the oppressors than with the victims. We know that in circumstances of torture, sometimes in those distorted, strange, inhuman conditions, people find themselves identifying with their torturers.

We also know that what happens at a broad level of society is that victims very easily become victimisers, turning the experience of the corruption of powerlessness, of being a victim, into the experience of having absolute power and abusing that power. If you think about one of the social groups in the twentieth century that has suffered most appallingly, if you think about the Jews, for example, a nice sense of human morality would say that people who suffered as the Jews collectively suffered during the Holocaust would then go on to become, in their dealings with others, the most ethical, the most moral group. Yet we know that this has not always been the case. We know that, in turn, many of the people who emerged from the Holocaust and founded the State of Israel perpetrated serious breaches of human rights against Palestinians. We know that Israel is one of the modern States that has practised torture. So there is no easy sense in which we learn the lessons of powerlessness. The experience of being powerless can transform itself into the experience of corrupt power.

We also know that in daily lives, in the lives of organisations, there can be a cycle of abuse and violence, where the abuse of power is reflected in a kind of chain of violence. We all know about the situation where the chairman of the company shouts at the CEO, the CEO abuses the deputy CEO, the deputy CEO insults the line manager, the line manager rages at the office manager, the office manager snaps at the secretary, the secretary gives out to the office boy and the office boy kicks the dog. That kind of cycle of the abuse of power again points us towards this sense in which the response to being powerless, or being in a situation of powerlessness in relation to somebody else, is very often one that in turn perpetuates a cycle of abuse.

What has all this got to do with modern Ireland? What I want to suggest very broadly is that in modern Ireland we know all about, or we should know all about, the corrupting effects of absolute powerlessness as well as the corrupting effects of absolute power.

We know – because we watch television, read the newspapers, listen to the radio discussions – what happens when power is not held accountable. But I think we also need to reflect on what happens in situations of powerlessness and how powerlessness itself can become a form of violence. The most extreme expression of this in modern Ireland is the IRA. If you think about the way in which the IRA in Northern Ireland, for example, transformed an experience of being an out-group, a group on the receiving end of corrupt power through all the years of unionist misrule in Northern Ireland, if you think about the transformation of that experience of powerlessness into, not a suggestion that there should be a new political morality but a determination to seize absolute power and use it against your enemies in a completely unaccountable and brutal way, then I think you have some sense of why we, particularly, should be aware of the way in which power can work. People who grow up in a society that does not value them, that does not offer them the amount of power that people need in order to be free citizens, can then turn themselves into the kind of people who are capable of walking into a fish shop on a Saturday afternoon and planting a bomb. It is something that is vivid, immediate and present to us. It is not an abstract reflection on the nature of power, but what we have seen throughout our own lives over the past thirty years.

But we could also think, for instance, of James Connolly's description of the wives of working men in early twentieth-century Ireland as the slaves of slaves, of the way in which very often in our family lives – particularly the old kind of family led by a powerful father – the humiliations of powerlessness inflicted on the husband were often in turn inflicted by the husband on the wife and children. Domestic violence, which is a very strong undercurrent in our society, is an arena in which we can understand and see and feel and taste the fear that is generated by powerlessness. What you get in these kinds of situations is the abuser, the inflicter of violence, being both the victim of absolute powerlessness and, in a different context, being the inflicter of absolute power. So there is not a simple sense in which there are powerful people and people without power. There is a much more complex continuum between those who have power and those who don't and the way in which that power is used.

One might think also of the horror of institutionalised child-abuse in Ireland, very often in Church-run industrial schools, a horror that this society is only beginning to face and to understand and that very early in the twenty-first century is going to be the first item on our agenda when the State establishes its commission on child-abuse. We are going to begin the twenty-first century hearing stories that will make our flesh creep and make us extremely depressed about ourselves. What I think we may begin to get to grips with, in hearing those stories, is again something about the complex nature of power. At a very obvious level, people who inflicted abuse on children in orphanages or industrial schools were classic cases of absolute power corrupting. They had the power to do what they liked and they did it. But – and this is perhaps where our society will come to some terms with what has happened – we can also probably see and will see that those people themselves were also in many cases the victims of absolute power, that they were shaped by powerlessness, that they were in institutional hierarchies where the primary value was absolute obedience and where their own personalities were misshapen and stunted by being in positions where they did not have the power to make free ethical choices. So I think in those stories, in a particularly disturbing and difficult but perhaps necessary process of enlightenment, we may see again the very complex and contradictory ways in which power works and in which powerlessness can be as corrupting as power.

One of the main reasons that I wanted to start talking about all of this, and looking at some of these very dark areas, is that it seems to me that it is critical for Irish society to avoid one of the most obvious kinds of mechanisms that are available to us at the moment. We are in a situation where we are suddenly experiencing, for the first time, a kind of economic power. We are in a situation where prosperity, which is a fundamental kind of social power, has descended on us in a quite unexpected and strange way, which we are still trying to come to terms with. Coinciding with that development of a certain kind of prosperity, we have a new awareness of corruption, a new awareness of the erosion of ethics, particularly in public life. Very often on the same news bulletin, item number one might be about new record figures in the economy, item number two might be about Charlie Haughey spending £16,000 on shirts, and item number three might be about the report of the trial of a religious brother on sex-abuse charges. So we are experiencing, in an existential, day-to-day way, some kind of feeling that there is a connection between prosperity and corruption, that the power that we have got as a society comes at the cost of the erosion of ethical standards.

And in that kind of situation, it is very tempting to turn back and say the problem is the prosperity, the problem is the development, the problem is wealth itself, and not something more complex, which is about the nature of power. It's very tempting for us to take refuge in a kind of nostalgia and to say that everything was fine when we were poor. We were poor but honest, we were poor but happy, and it is only now that we are developing as a society that we have these ethical problems. Mired as we are in all sorts of scandals, it is very tempting to invent a simpler, nicer place, which was not corrupt because it was not prosperous.

I think what that ignores is the corrupting effects of powerlessness, it ignores the extent to which we were corrupted not by power, but by powerlessness, and the extent to which that had a very important shaping effect on the kind of society out of which we have emerged.

It is very important therefore to remember that the past was not some kind of ethical paradise, that the Ireland of the thirties, forties, fifties and sixties was not a place without very fundamental problems in terms of its social and personal ethics and its idea of public morality. I don't think anybody, realistically looking back, could now say that the way in which we treated the most vulnerable in Irish society, such as children who were institutionalised, spoke very highly for our sense of ethics as a society. I don't think anybody, looking back on the hiring fairs where labourers, often little more than children, stood around waiting to be hired by farmers to work as labourers (something that was seen at the time by most people as being comparable to the way in which slaves were sold in the southern states of the United States in the early nineteenth century), could say that it was a paradise of ethics to which we should return. I don't think anyone who looks at the way in which the Irish society out of which we came constructed essentially a kind of social bargain that allowed us to maintain a relatively conservative, relatively static society at the cost of mass emigration – so that the people who emigrated could bear the cost of protecting the lifestyle of those who remained at home – could realistically say that that was an ethical social choice.

I say these things not to deny that there were wonderful things about the Ireland from which we have come – there were very many examples of fundamental decency and kindness and compassion and there were great forces of creativity and intelligence within that society. But it was no simpler than the society in which we live in terms of the kinds of moral choices it made, and we cannot understand ourselves by reference to a supposed golden age, when everything was more innocent. The nature of corruption was different, the things we were corrupt about were perhaps somewhat different, and while what we are seeing now is on the one hand disturbing and disheartening, it is also heartening for one fundamental reason, which is that we are seeing it, it is being spoken about, it is on display. That process of opening up what had been closed, of speaking about what had been silent is a very disturbing and difficult and painful process for most of us. But it is a process that I think is much healthier, and in the long term much more ethical, than a process of concealment, of not speaking and of not acknowledging, which I think was very often what happened in the society we came out of.

So it is not a simple question of saying that Irish society has been corrupted by development or has been made less ethical by the fact that it is wealthier. The erosion of ethics that we are seeing is I think quite specific and quite precisely placed in the process of Irish development. One of the key things about the society from which we are emerging and about the scandals that we are seeing daily is that they are not scandals that arise from being a prosperous society, they are scandals that arise very largely from the process of *becoming* a prosperous society. They are scandals that arise from a period of fundamental transition, and I think we have to understand them in that context and understand the ethical problems that they pose in the context of a very fundamental and rapidly changing society.

It seems to me that, although we can never make very dogmatic judgements about these things, it probably is true to say that both political and business life in Ireland up to the 1960s was more ethical in certain respects than it is now. There are very obvious and fundamental reasons why that should be so. In the first place, it is not that people were nicer or better, because I think anybody who looks at history has a sense that human nature changes relatively little. What changes are the circumstances in which it is expressed and there were very fundamental changes of circumstance in the emergencies of modern Ireland.

What you had in most of the history of this State were two very powerful ethical restraints on the behaviour of people who had power in the economic sphere or in the political sphere. Those restraints were politics and faith. We do know that for most of the people who established this State, there was a genuine and fundamental sense of idealism. That idealism may have been naive, it may have been distorted, it may have been wrongly expressed in all sorts of ways, but I think few people would seriously question its existence. Certainly for the first generation of Irish leaders in politics and business, and I think probably for the second and third generation to some extent, by virtue of the fact that they were still quite close in generational terms to that founding moment, there was a sense that the building of a nation, the building of a society was in itself a reward. This is not to say that these leaders did not enjoy exercising power, that they did not enjoy the relative privileges that came from being in a position of power. But it is a remarkable contrast to look at the wills left by senior politicians who had opportunities for graft, and who clearly did not take them. If you look at the circumstances in which somebody like Seán Lemass, for example, died, the kind of will he left, his was a fairly modest, prosperous, middle-class lifestyle. He seems to have aspired to a middle-class lifestyle and nothing much beyond that. The contrast between that and the lifestyle of his son-in-law does not need to be emphasised.

One of the powerful forces behind this was the notion that these people were part of a social project and that the project itself, whether it was the right project or the wrong project, constrained people's behaviour and gave them a sense that they had obligations to others that went far beyond the personal. I think it is probably true that for almost all of those people who served in government up to the 1960s, there was at least a sense in the back of their minds that they were contributing towards the building of a young nation, that if they could go to their graves with a sense that they had contributed to that, then they had fulfilled one of the fundamental ambitions of power.

By contrast, one of the forces that has operated to break this idealism down is the large process through which, for example, the word ideology has become a term of abuse in politics. The early generations of Irish politicians were fundamentally ideological. They were nationalists. They had a sense of a project and they believed in that project. Sometime around the late 1960s, the accusation that somebody was ideologically driven became an insult. To suggest that somebody was motivated ideologically, which after all is simply the same thing as having a vision and having a project, was somehow to disqualify them from politics. We pushed ourselves in a direction of valuing a kind of pragmatism, a short-termism, a sense of getting things done, of immediate achievement. Let it be said that this was probably a necessary corrective to what had gone before. But it gradually gathered around itself the feeling that it could be a justification for everything. The atmosphere changed very fundamentally and the restraint of nation-building – the restraint that you felt you had an obligation to the wider society – was gradually eroded, particularly as nationalism, often for very good reasons, became less of a potent force in Irish society.

The other big restraint on people, of course, was religion. Strange as it may seem, very many people in the public world and in the business world did have a sense of religious obligation. Again, that sense of religious obligation may have been driven by hypocrisy, may have been less sincere than it seemed to be. It may also not have operated all the time, in the way it should. It probably did operate through the fact that they were afraid of burning in hell, and that can be a very important restraint on people's activities.

Clearly that fundamental sense of religious attachment, and particularly of religious punishment – the idea that there will be a kind of summary justice at the end of your life even if you evade it throughout the course of your life – has very fundamentally eroded in Irish society, as in every other Western society. It is part of the modernising process, it happens when societies become secularised, urban and modern, and it has happened to us in exactly the same way as everybody else.

But what I want to suggest is that through those two things, we have lost the restraints that were there on certain kinds of behaviour. What is important for us to understand is that this process of erosion is not entirely a process that is due to the emergence of a very wealthy society. It is also due to the erosion of certain things that inhered in the old society but do not necessarily belong to the emerging new society. It belongs to a period of transition in which you lose the old restraints and you haven't gained any new ones. You get a period when everything is up for grabs, when the only kind of compass that people have for the use of power is self-interest and a short-term sense of self-aggrandisement.

Now you can regret that process, you can be nostalgic about what went before, you can decry what has happened since, but we have to recognise that change was inevitable and may ultimately lead to, of all things, a much more deeply rooted sense of ethics and morality.

The fundamental weakness of the old system of public ethics from which we have come is that it was imposed from the top down. It did not depend on people making free choices but on people having no choice. It was imposed in a way that said there is a social consensus and if you go outside of this you will be punished. You may be punished in this life or you may be punished in the next life, but you can be sure that you will be punished in one form or another. It was therefore a process that depended very largely on the creation of a kind of coercive situation. It depended on a kind of powerlessness, on people not having the power to make real decisions about how to behave. That kind of system could function very effectively in a closed society, because you could control what would happen to people and what would not happen to them. You could control information, you could control ideas and you could control imagery.

But one way or another, that kind of coercive morality was going to disappear, as the society changed and as the twentieth century moved on. It was fundamentally impossible under any circumstances to maintain a closed society in Ireland, and with that impossibility comes the fact that the system of public ethics that existed was simply not going to last. What was probably always going to happen in that kind of situation was that, as the whole system collapsed, you would have a free-for-all. You would have a period in which people felt able to do whatever they wanted. For what had existed were only the restraints, rather than the deep and fundamental sense of responsibility. What you didn't have was a free choice to behave ethically. People had behaved ethically because they didn't have any choice. Increasingly, when choice became available, what happened to us was that there was a simple absence of restraint, an absence of reasons not to behave in these kinds of ways. What we saw and what we have seen is wholescale and massive indulgence in unethical behaviour.

I think it should also be said that one of the fundamental weaknesses of the system of public morality that we had was that it concentrated much more on the private sphere than on the public sphere. It was far more interested in talking about what happened in bedrooms than what happened in boardrooms. It was far more directed towards private behaviour between consenting adults than towards the idea of a society and of social obligation. That is not to deny that there were very elaborate and powerful social elements in, for example, Catholic teaching. But in terms of the way in which that teaching was transmitted and received, its impact was mostly on private behaviour. It proved fatally weak at inculcating a sense of public morality.

So if we are going to get ourselves out of the situation we are in at the moment and if we are going to construct a new public morality, it is very important that we get the order in which things have happened right. We have to be clear that it is not prosperity that has eroded ethics. On the contrary, it's the erosion of ethics that has determined the *nature* of our prosperity. What I mean by that is that the major impact of unethical behaviour on the development of the kind of society that we now have is how it has determined who would be in and who would be out in a prosperous society. It determined the nature of the prosperity and how that prosperity would be shared. So it was the fact that we had a lack of public morality that shaped the kind of prosperity we have; it was not the prosperity that shaped the lack of public morality.

This happened in very concrete and precise ways. The key period in the development of contemporary Irish society was the period between the late 1980s and early 1990s. It was in that period that the question of who would have power and who would not have power in the Ireland of 1999 was essentially decided. You had a society that was going through a traumatic process of social, political and economic adjustment. This was the period in which Irish society was at a kind of a crossroads, where there were serious doubts about whether the modern project was going to work at all in Ireland, where the multinational companies were pulling out, where the national debt was mounting to massive and unsustainable levels, where the viability of the Irish economic project was very seriously and substantially in doubt. That is the period in which Irish society had to reshape itself and reposition itself in the world economy and to create the possibility for the kind of economic success that exists now.

What is critical and tragic is that it was also the time at which the erosion of public ethics was at its most sharp, most appalling and most vulgar. That is the period in which we lost the restraints on the behaviour of people in power, while having no mechanism for recreating any kind of new public restraints. We did not have public ethics legislation, we did not have freedom of information, we did not have any limits on the abuse of money in politics, and we did not have any limits on the ways in which business could influence public life. The limits we have now are seriously inadequate but at least they exist. During that period we were at our most vulnerable, if you like, in terms of being open to the abuse of power. And that was the period in which the loss of any sense of ethical restraint on the part of very significant sections of Irish society was at its most strong.

What essentially happened in that period is something quite astonishing. Very significant sections of the political and business elite withdrew their allegiance from the State. Quite simply, a very significant group of the leadership of Irish society decided that it had no obligations to that society whatsoever. We know that there was massive tax evasion, we know that many people in positions of power and influence and authority had more loyalty to the Cayman Islands than to Ireland. We know that this happened in a way that included a very large degree of collusion between many of the bodies who would be assumed to sustain a certain notion of ethical conduct in public life. We know that things like the Ansbacher scam or the massive evasion of dirt tax, for instance, would not have been possible without either the tacit collusion or the active collusion of banks, building societies, solicitors, accountants and professional people in general. Every one of those groups had professional associations with codes of ethics, which they were supposed to adhere to. We know that, with a number of very honourable exceptions, by and large those groups did not apply their own ethics. So you had a situation in which the concrete codes of ethics, which were, I suppose, the secular equivalent of the old Church-based rules and orders for how to behave, were certainly no more powerful than the older restraints had been and perhaps in many ways less powerful. But the effect of that was to shape kinds of prosperity in which there would be winners and losers. The function of the corruption was to ensure first of all that in the very difficult process of social adjustment, those who were able to buy their way out of having to bear the burden could do so.

2

THE HUMAN DIMENSION IN THE WORKPLACE

Catherine McGeachy

Why should we bother with the human dimension in our workplaces? With such forces as e-commerce, will we need to focus on people at all? Certainly, the statistics for e-commerce are compelling: according to Dr Andy Grove, chairman of Intel, e-commerce is here to stay. All companies that are going to operate in the economies of a few years in the future will be Internet companies. Certainly, the percentage of US GDP on the Internet in 1999 has been less than 1 per cent. However, by 2003, that figure will jump to 10 per cent. In 1997, the percentage of Intel's business performed on the Internet was zero. In 1998, that figure had risen to 20 per cent, representing $5.25 billion, and in 1999, the figure has shot to 40 per cent, representing $12.0 billion. Andersen Consulting]see figure 1] reflect these figures in their identification of new and continuing imperatives for business: revenue growth through retention of customers and expansion of product and service offerings; e-commerce, through launching new e-business and extension of channels onto the Internet; mergers and acquisitions, and cost reduction. So, why, given this information, should the 'millennium organisation' put energy into developing the human dimension in its workplace?

According to Andersen Consulting, a recent survey by *The Economist's* Intelligence Unit ranked human performance ahead of productivity and technology as a source of competitive strength. In the same survey, the ability to attract and retain the best people is predicted to be the primary force influencing business strategy by 2005. *The Harvard Business Review* documents why this is so. In their case-study of Sears Roebuck, one of the world's largest retailers, they

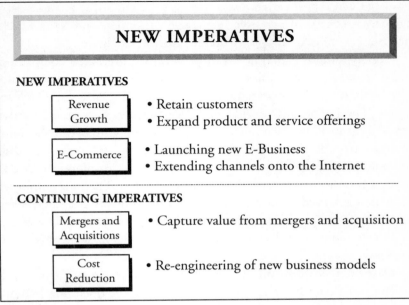

Figure 1

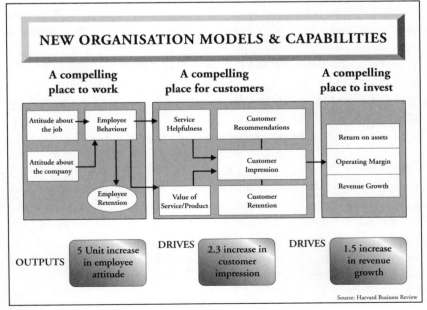

Figure 2

have claimed that for every 5-unit increase in employee attitude, you can drive in excess of a twofold increase in customer impression, which drives a 1.5 times increase in revenue growth [see figure 2].

The hypothesis is that if you make your organisation a compelling place to work, it becomes a compelling place for customers and ultimately turns the organisation into a compelling place in which to invest. The hypothesis consists of three interlinked modules. Firstly, create a compelling place to work by focusing on employee behaviour through attitude about the job and the company. The effort in this module typically generates a 5-unit increase in employee attitude. Secondly, create a compelling place for customers. The new employee behaviour achieved in module one drives service helpfulness, perceived value of service/product and customer recommendations. The effort in this module typically generates a 2.3-unit increase in customer impression.

Customer impression drives customer recommendation and retention, which ultimately drives return on assets, operating margin and a 1.5-unit increase in revenue growth. This is the third of the interlinked modules: create a compelling place to invest. This is achieved by focusing on return on assets, operating margin and revenue growth. But, the foundation for this growth is creating a compelling place to work.

Harvard research indicates that to focus properly on model one, the compelling place to work, an organisation has to focus on its intellectual capital – its people. Intellectual capital is developed by making people competent and committed, and by allowing and helping them to converge and operate as a team.

Competence
Through excellent selection processes, you buy in the best talent and build on this talent by training and developing the employees; you borrow talent when necessary; you 'bounce out' talent that is not congruent with the team and the values of the organisation, and you bind talent to the organisation. This is achieved through generating commitment [see figure 3].

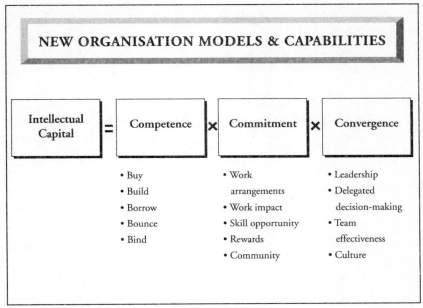

Figure 3

Commitment

Talent will stay with an organisation if there are flexible work arrangements. Many of our large organisations have successfully explored the use of the 'virtual office' concept. Boeing's scheme reveals a 15 to 30 per cent increase in productivity, with zero staff turnover. British Telecom have dramatically reduced turnover through enabling 24,000 employees to work remotely. In the UK generally, more than one million employees are working from home. This number is growing by 200,000 per annum.

Showing employees how their work impacts the growth of the business and interconnects with other colleagues, providing skill opportunities and performance-related rewards to employees, and building in the organisation a sense of community, each play their part in generating in employees a sense of commitment. Interestingly, the Harvard research points to the building of community as a central 'gluing' agent:

Creating a Sense of Community in the Workplace
There are two ways in which a sense of community can be created in

the workplace: building spirituality at work and removing fear from the workplace.

1. Building Spirituality at Work

Why is there an interest in this subject? Firstly, while corporate downsizing and greater demands on remaining workers have left them too tired and stressed to be creative, globalisation of markets requires more creativity from employees. Secondly, to survive the twenty-first century, research is showing that organisations must offer a greater sense of meaning and purpose for their workforce. Thirdly, in today's highly competitive environment, the best talents seek out organisations that reflect their inner values and provide opportunities for personal development and community service – not just bigger salaries. A good example of this is David Cole, former group executive of America Online. He says that he had a long list of things he would never do for a living. For example, he wouldn't promote products that had an inbuilt planned obsolescence (which he said covered almost everything he saw in America); he wouldn't work for a company peddling junk, nor for a company that promoted pesticides.

Is spirituality important to employees? People increasingly want to bring a greater sense of meaning and purpose into their worklives. They want their work to reflect their personal mission in life, according to Corinne McLaughlin, executive director at the Center for Visionary Leadership in San Francisco. Dr Ernst Volgenau, founder, president and CEO of the highly successful systems development organisation SRA, worked with the US Secretary of Defence analysing and developing large technological systems before setting up his own hugely successful company. He comments that as an engineer, he wanted to set up a company that would use technology to solve societal problems, rather than just existing as a technology company. He told himself that he would like to have a company that mirrored his interests. According to a *USA Weekend* poll held in July 1998, spirituality is cited as the second most important factor in personal happiness (after health) by 47 per cent of Americans questioned. David Cole comments that as a director in the company Software Plus he was amazed that almost all of the employees shared the same spiritual belief system, and this really helped them in their relationships with one another. He could see the value for the employees of having a unified worldview, and how the employees needed a larger connection in order to achieve their potential as a group.

Are spirituality and profitability mutually exclusive? According to Professor Verschoor of the University of Chicago, companies with a defined corporate commitment to ethical principles do better than companies that don't make ethics a key management component. According to the Wilson Learning Company in the US, 39 per cent of the variability in corporate performance is attributable to the personal satisfaction of the staff. Ernst Volgenau, president of SRA, says that, for his company, 'Honesty means more than simply complying with the law. It means maintaining a high ethical framework . . . you must view employees as valued assets and then you must treat them with the personal dignity and respect that they're entitled to as individuals. If you do that, it's a smart business decision. On the other hand, if you choose to treat them like chattel, or like interchangeable parts, they'll contribute as if they are. For the most part, people will give you what you deserve.' *Business Week* notes that 39 per cent of US investors say they always or frequently check on business practices, values and ethics before investing, and *The Trends Report* of 1997 documents that three out of four consumers polled say they are likely to switch brands associated with a good cause if price and quality are equal. *Business Week* discovered that 95 per cent of Americans reject the idea that a corporation's only purpose is to make money.

How is spirituality manifesting in the workplace? In four broad ways. Firstly, more employers are encouraging spirituality as a way to boost loyalty and enhance morale, as can be seen from the proliferation of book titles such as: *Soul of Business; Liberating the Corporate Soul; Working From the Heart; The Stirring of Soul in the Workplace; Spirit at Work; Jesus CEO; Redefining the Corporate Soul; The Corporate Mystic; Leading with Soul.* Secondly, there are several American newsletters on spirituality at work; several Internet newsgroups on spirituality at work and, last year alone, there were twenty conferences on the subject in the US. Thirdly, according to ABC Evening News, growing numbers of business people want to bring their whole selves to work – body, mind and spirit. The

American Stock Exchange has a Torah study group, Boeing has Christian, Jewish and Muslim prayer groups and Microsoft has an on-line prayer service. Spiritual study groups at noon are sometimes called 'higher power lunches' instead of the usual 'power lunches'. Fourthly, employers are clarifying the company vision and mission and aligning these with a higher purpose and deeper commitment to service to both customers and community. David Cole of America Online comments: 'My view is that we need to redefine principal to include our own planet, which means that we can think about spending non-renewable resources, but let's account for them and know what we're doing. Capitalism isn't completely broken. It simply fails to account for the real costs of many enterprises.'

The means by which spirituality is manifest in the workplace is typically through three routes: firstly, the embodying of personal values of honesty, integrity, kindness, thoughtfulness, patience, co-operativeness, forgiveness and good quality of work; secondly, treating employees in a responsible, caring way; thirdly, making the organisation socially responsible for how it impacts the environment, serves the community and creates social change. How spirituality manifests in the workplace can take many forms. These are: prayer and scripture study; meditation; centring exercises such as deep breathing to reduce stress; visioning exercises; building shared values; active, deep listening; making action and intention congruent; using intuition and inner guidance in decision-making.

2. Removing Fear from the Workplace

The second way of building a sense of community in the workplace is by removing fear from the workplace. When Professor Stephen Hawking, the renowned physicist, discovered an intelligent particle in the atom, which interacts with the subconscious expectations of the observer, causing the intelligent particle to bring to the observer exactly what that observer expects, he created one of the greatest watersheds in our thinking this century. Negative dispositions would, therefore, attract to themselves other negative dispositions and outcomes, and positive dispositions would attract other positive dispositions and outcomes. This powerful discovery meant that individuals would have to learn to take responsibility for their inner dispositions and the outcomes they were bringing to them and to those in their circle.

In her bestselling book, *Leadership and the New Science*, Dr Margaret Wheatley, consultant to many blue-chip companies, shows how revolutionary discoveries in quantum physics, chaos theory and biology are overturning centuries-old images of the universe and providing powerful insights into the design, leadership and management of organisations. Dr Wheatley asks, 'How is order different than control?', 'How would focusing on relationships enhance your organisation?', 'Give examples of how your organisation inspires individuals to give their lives meaning.' Dr Wheatley is actively experimenting with organisational redesigns that support the speed, flexibility, resilience and autonomy required in today's environment. But she reminds us that physicists have discovered that thought patterns generate force fields – morphogenic fields – that literally hang invisibly in space, impacting the thoughts of those who come within their orbit and, according to Rupert Sheldrake, one of the world's leading biologists, when a thought pattern is adopted by a sufficient number of people (i.e., a critical mass), it transports over to the whole group, who will adopt the thought pattern as a norm!

What does all this mean? It means that the thoughts we think are affecting other people, their performance at work and their view of themselves and what they are capable of achieving. We have often heard the old proverbs 'Birds of a feather flock together' and 'Success breeds success'. Margaret Wheatley's research proves that the quality of thinking of those in leadership positions dramatically affects the levels of thinking of those they lead.

Armed with this information, why is it that our organisations are not examining more thoroughly the quality of thinking taking place in their workplaces, and 'cleaning up' the thinking of their leaders and employees by training on the dangers of thinking negatively and how to think constructively in every situation with every person? As Dr Hans Selye, one of the pioneers of stress management, points out, stress and problems are out there. It's how we respond to the stressors and problems that creates or avoids stress. Given that the quality of our thinking determines the quality of our performance, organisations should look at those areas and people in the organisation that spark negative thinking in their employees and help leaders and employees to develop appropriate interventions to deal with them.

How can an organisation remove fear from the workplace? In three ways. Firstly, look again at your communications processes. Does your organisation encourage feedback without repercussions? Many people tell me that they cannot say what is really on their minds because of the mild to hugely negative reaction from the person to whom they speak. People have told me of their superior reacting so personally to feedback that they have been victimised in terms of promotion, bonuses, work conditions such as type of car allowed, type of office/equipment allowed, when they could go on holidays, etc. This is tantamount to bullying and certainly does not foster a sense of community at work. I have known talented individuals, seriously contributing to the financial success of their companies, who have chosen to leave their companies and set up the same business for themselves, bringing some of the organisation's clientele with them. Why? Because they finally couldn't take the constant repression of their views. If your organisation allows such low-level communication, consider the commercial and time costs of losing the experience of the talented individual, the time needed to recruit and select a replacement, the time for the new person to find their feet and the cost of the lost clientele. Creating a culture in which people are free to say what is on their mind is not just a junior management basic, it is an organisational essential.

Often complaints and negative feedback are like free consultancy: they show the organisation better ways of handling a situation. More importantly, allowing employees to say what is on their minds without a negative backlash removes the sense of isolation that the negative backlash creates. Honest, open feedback that is sincerely received and considered is a hallmark of a healthy relationship and creates a sense of inclusiveness. Has your organisation been alienating or including its people?

Another aspect of removing fear in the communication process is the ability to actively draw out different views on a situation. I recently undertook a job for a company in which the marketing director thought that the only way of considering the company's vision and values was from the marketing point of view. This is the kind of limited thinking that David Cole of America Online did away with using an innovative mentoring system. He says, 'We hire a lot of really smart young people and, rather than telling them what to do, we tell them what problems we're grappling with and we ask them "How would you approach this?" We learn so much more that way. These young people in our company are some of the best people in the industry and they weren't even in the industry last year. But they have this passion and they have great intellects and they're curious. Their eyes sparkle. They have lots of different ways of dealing with things. So, I tell people when I recruit them – "If you really want to learn twice as fast as your competitors, find a mentor half your age." ' Again, on the business of actively seeking different views on a situation, David Cole comments, 'Too many really smart people out there – chief executives – only want the answers. They don't understand that while they can be faster than all of their employees, if they don't include them in that process of searching for the answers, in the end they're going to be slower than their competitors.'

A third aspect of removing fear from the communications process is to encourage appreciation of difference. In today's global business where complexities are common, applying many views to a discussion and decision is critical. This can be difficult to achieve because of the perceived knowledge/education base of the contributors and the view of some contributors that such discussions are their preserve. History tells us that great ideas come from the edges of a system, not from the system's core, which is often too close to the situation to see it in all its aspects. For example, the diving bell was invented by an astronomer, Edmund Halley; the pneumatic tyre was invented by a vet, John Dunlop; the safety razor was invented by a salesman, King Camp Gillette. Then there are those too close in their expertise to see the wood from the trees. Thomas Edison, on electricity in the home, said, 'Just as certain as death, Westinghouse will kill a customer within six months after he puts in a system of any size'; physicist Lord Kelvin said 'X-rays are a hoax, radio has no future', and *The Science Digest* of August 1948 commented that 'Landing and moving around on the moon offer so many serious problems for human beings that it may take science another 200 years to lick them'!

Tormod Byork, metallurgist and senior vice-president of Global Business and Project Development at Norway's 'Hydro Aluminium' plant, found an innovative way to encourage appreciation of difference in his organisation and ensure that all aspects of an issue were considered and respected by all parties. He came up with a garden metaphor in order to enhance productivity, cut costs and encourage employee involvement and motivation. Each plant in the garden represented one of the business units: finished products were berries; customers became the birds and the bees; the sales and marketing people ended up being the smell from the flowers. The leaves told how the organisation functions. Tormod Byork says, 'We couldn't communicate very well because we didn't have a common language. A lawyer speaks a totally different language from that of an economist. Even among engineers a metallurgist has a totally different language compared to an electrical engineer. The metaphor of the garden liberated us from our boxes and brought us together.'

After communication, the second way of removing fear from the workplace and so creating a sense of community is to check the 'disposition' of the organisation. To check the disposition of the organisation, find out what employees are picturing in their minds – is it positive or negative? The pictures in our minds govern our behaviour and control our level of motivation. Motivation is ultimately an internally driven factor. As long as the organisation engages in externally driven motivational inputs to its employees, it disempowers them. Often I see plaques on walls espousing the vision and mission of the organisation. That plaque represents the picture of the organisation in the minds of a few only. Mostly, the employees have a different picture in their minds and it is this picture – broken though it may be – that is driving their day-to-day performance.

Ask employees what makes the disposition of the organisation subdued. Train employees to take responsibility for their own inner state because thoughts create realities, as we have seen from quantum theory. Consider whether employees are operating as functions or as human beings in functions. Do employees feel they are part of a community that values them? Are employees aware that their thoughts affect their colleagues mentally and physically and the general working atmosphere?

Apart from the work of Stephen Hawking and Rupert Sheldrake, a research team at the University of Paris, led by physicist Alain Aspect, discovered in 1982 that under certain circumstances electrons are able to communicate instantaneously with each other regardless of the distance separating them. It didn't matter whether the particles were ten feet or ten billion miles apart. Somehow each particle always seemed to know what the other was doing. This research corroborates Rupert Sheldrake's work that thought impacts, positively or negatively, the person or object transmitted to. The work of Sheldrake and many others proves that negative thoughts alone directed towards a person weaken that person physically and mentally. Is it any wonder we have so much depression and non-specific illness in our workplaces, costing hundreds of thousands of pounds in lost labour? It is time we made individuals at all levels of the organisation responsible for the outcome of their thoughts.

Are employees having fun? David Firth, author of *How to Make Work Fun,* comments, 'We spend 41 per cent of our waking hours at work. Since we're asleep for a further 35 per cent, it seems crazy to consign "life" and with it any hope of fun to the remaining 24 per cent. Why do we leave our personalities behind when we set off for work in the morning? Why do we envy people who tell us that their work is fun, yet somehow feel laughter is out of place in the office? And how can we deliver excellent service or be better than our competitors if we would rather not be working at all?'

In my experience, I see an average working day of twelve hours, sometimes for six days a week, developing in many companies. In one company, the young men in a workshop I was facilitating lamented that they had no time to 'spot the talent', those who had entered the company with a girlfriend had no time to get engaged, those who had entered the company engaged had no time to get married, those who entered the company married had no time to have a family, and those with a family had very little time with their family. In other words, they were describing a systematic dismantling of the building blocks of our future society and the repressing of a basic human instinct: finding a mate. To me, this is a time-bomb waiting to explode and is one of the reasons employees are choosing to work for themselves and even work from home.

The third way of removing fear from the workplace and generating a practical sense of community with people caring for one another is by redesigning the organisation's appraisal/performance management system. For example, people do what they are measured on in order to succeed. In your organisation, do you measure employees on how well an employee fosters a constructive atmosphere or on how co-operative an employee is with colleagues or on how much initiative an employee takes to help colleagues?

A constructive, co-operative employee who takes initiatives to help colleagues is going to create a sense of community and a sense of employees being valued. But we rarely factor in these elements in appraisal and performance management systems, which favour more the basic criteria of teamwork, time management and communications. Yes, these criteria should leave room for the co-operative and constructive, but mostly they don't.

So, personally, I have experienced companies in which the performance management system pitches employees against one another by asking them to comment on one another in a salary- and bonus-linked measurement system. People have told me there is no way that they would be honest in their appraisal of their colleagues because if they gave their colleagues a good rating, their colleagues would possibly get a better bonus than they would or the concerned colleague might not even get a bonus because, in some systems, in a group of twenty only ten get a bonus.

We have performance management systems in many of our companies, which are designed in countries in which there is no general living experience of *meitheal* – the Gaelic sense of a community helping one another out – and, therefore, these countries have designed systems that force competitive performance to get the results they want. In Ireland, on the other hand, we have the living and successful experience of *meitheal*, where people are naturally, culturally encoded to help their fellow man and woman, getting great results in the process. Yet we have cut across this, ignored it and the enormous gains it brings, and trained our people to be self-centred and to engage in unhealthy individualism.

Convergence

Finally, the third module of intellectual capital – the human dimension at work – is convergence. This is about helping people to operate as a team through proper leadership, delegated decision-making, team effectiveness and a culture that supports its intellectual capital. David Cole of America Online comments, 'You've got to start with the big picture – look at vision, values and core competencies. Values must be inculcated throughout the company and relentlessly practised at the top. Even if you have a company that's a $2 billion global company, if you don't answer the first question about who you are and what your relationship is to the rest of the universe, you'll find yourself in a precarious position.' In terms of leadership, he continues, 'We are investing in building a new kind of entrepreneur, one who really knows how to build teams and create new business explicitly oriented towards yielding dual dividends – dividends in the traditional sense of return on capital and also in the sense of what's sustainable and good for the community.'

Conclusion

Intellectual capital is developed by helping employees to be competent, committed and team-driven. Each of these three elements works interdependently and each reflects an environment that supports people, because ultimately it is people who will mastermind E-Commerce and the companies of the future; it is people who will put a brake on or drive the bottom line, and without the right people we will not be able to create the new organisation models required to survive in the future. We must build the human dimension in the workplace.

A VIEW FROM THE CHAIR

CIARAN LYNCH

This session consisted of two presentations, one by Fintan O'Toole and the other by Catherine McGeachy. Both presentations were interesting and challenging. They made us consider and address issues that are close to our sense of ourselves and to our view of reality.

Fintan O'Toole addressed the issues of power and powerlessness in our society and the extent to which they have impacted on public ethics. He proposed that the founding fathers of the State and their immediate successors were driven by a sense of public duty and public morality that put the common good above self-interest. This, he believed, arose from a number of factors including the power of religion and the ideals that flourished in the State's emergence from conflict. He proposed that this started to change around the 1970s when self-interest began to become more important than the public interest, and that much of our present-day scandals were traceable to this change of focus, which was reflective not of economic success but of the transition from poverty to wealth. He also focused on the extent to which powerlessness as well as power gives opportunities for non-ethical actions, since powerlessness erodes the sense of personal responsibility.

Catherine McGeachy focused on optimum behaviour within the organisation. She emphasised recent research which suggests that positive thinking and positive attitudes have a physiological effect that can impact on the effectiveness of the individual and the organisation. She also focused on the extent to which non-financial rewards are important in optimising the output of a firm's workforce as well as delivering a sense of well-being to the worker.

Both presentations were very well received by the audience, in different ways. Fintan O'Toole's presentation seemed to strike a chord of recognition in many participants, who felt that it gave an explanation and a context for many of the public revelations that are taking place today. Catherine McGeachy's presentation, on the other hand, challenged people's sense of reality. Her proposition, based on the impact of sub-atomic particles on human behaviour, that the interests of the individual and the organisation can best be served by similar organisational patterns, drew a more disbelieving response but gave rise to a lot of reflection.

It is difficult to draw coherent threads from two such disparate presentations, one with a broad historical sweep and a close cultural reference, the other with a much more specific focus, drawing much reference from research in the US. However, the following occurred to me during the course of the presentations. Both presentations spoke of the importance of being aware of the existence of a world beyond ourselves, of a transcendental element to our lives. Fintan spoke of the influence of this in ensuring that an ethic which sees more than self-interest forms the basis of our public decision-making, while Catherine spoke of it in terms of the effect that each of us has on others and the need to be aware of this and to behave accordingly. Such an awareness needs to permeate our lives in the political, communal and organisational spheres.

Both spoke of the need for our actions to have meaning and to be related to norms of behaviour and shared values. Fintan spoke of the need for us to build shared values to replace or modify those that we shared in the past. Catherine spoke of this in the context of the need for the workforce in an organisation to share the vision and mission of the organisation. I was reminded of the work of Durkheim, one of the founding fathers of sociology, who said that a society where the structure of norms and values was weak was one in which the meaninglessness of life was greatest and one where suicidal behaviour would be most marked. I think we were challenged by these papers to reflect on the extent to which agreed value systems now exist in our society.

Both also focused on the mechanisms that might be used in reaching the decisions with which their papers were concerned. Fintan referred to the importance of decisions not being made in a top-down prescriptive way. To me he was saying that we would get a system as good as the effort that we were willing to put into creating it. Catherine was more focused on the mechanisms that might be used in the organisation to develop a sense of corporate loyalty. It occurred to me that the nature of the mechanisms can be as critical as their focus. A moderately good decision reached through a good mechanism might well be more appropriate than a better decision reached through a poor mechanism.

It appeared to me that all of these issues ultimately come together around the concept of participation. The methods of participation that we develop, the extent to which we are willing to use those mechanisms and their acceptance by the decision-makers will have a major influence on how we develop as individuals and as a society. Perhaps the ills that were referred to by Fintan and the optimum organisational behaviour referred to by Catherine stem at least in part from the nature of participation in decision-making that has occurred in the past.

Good participation requires knowledge, opportunity, ability and willingness to be involved. The provision of appropriate structures for participation will be to no avail if the knowledge required and the ability to participate are not also developed. Conferences such as this and the work done by organisations such as LEADER in developing the ability of communities to participate in the management of the development of their own communities are important elements in giving people the knowledge, power and willingness to participate. If we are to have organisations that are truly sustaining of themselves and of their members, if we are to have a society in which power and powerlessness do not exist in parallel, then the mechanisms of participation that we develop will be of critical importance.

As a final comment I would like to refer to the degree to which the participants in the conference involved themselves in the sessions. The response to the request for silence for a period of reflection before and after the presentations was wonderful and the way in which people wrote down their responses was also exemplary. The wish to participate in the discussion at the end was widespread, which indicated the extent to which the speakers had touched the audience, and there were many who were still waiting to address questions to the speakers when the session drew to a close.

UPDATE ON APPLIED RESEARCH CENTRE AND OTHER DEVELOPMENTS

Harry Bohan

Last year's conference, 'Are We Forgetting Something?', underlined the fact that Irish society was experiencing unprecedented change. The country is experiencing unparalleled economic growth, bringing with it a welcome increase in prosperity and material well-being. We are now heavily influenced by the global culture, transnational technology and corporations specialising in telecommunications, computers and data processing. All of this suggests that we live in an information age. In a sense, that is a myth; rather, we live in a media age, and that is a different thing. In many ways, the media has never before held such sway. However, in the media's global village, the majority of real people do not feature. At best, they are mere consumers. In Britain only 3 per cent of peak-time programmes feature anything about the majority of humanity.

Leaders – political, religious, sporting – tend to be very much pawns of the media. It is important to say what is politically correct and to put a spin on the message. Leaders tend to be led by public opinion and moral courage is in short supply. Massive resources are invested in researching and producing the global product or message. Old loyalties and signposts such as organised religion, party politics, belonging to people and place, family and community are falling on hard times.

A clear message from last year's conference was that globalisation and modernisation need to be balanced. What are the issues concerning people – where they are – that give meaning to life? Global economics needs to be humanised, integrating the corporation and the community. What is happening to the family? Market values shape us, but what about spiritual values, the power of voluntarism? These and other issues were all highlighted.

In short, the clear message was: There are signs that when a society decides to fly on one wing, namely, that of economic success, the fall-out can be serious. It can be serious for the elderly, for the young, for relationships. Grave questions of injustice may need answering and there is the question too of displacement, which sees 40 per cent of the population of Ireland now living in the greater Dublin area. Major ethical issues have loomed in our society. In the face of all this change, there is a real danger that people lose sight of what inspires and unites them. When structures, institutions and corporations so dominate society, we can forget that they exist *for* people. Society then loses its soul and words like community and spirituality lose their meaning.

So, an Applied Research Centre was founded in the past year in response to the need to restore a sense of balance. It evolved naturally from an organisation with over twenty-five years of experience in local development, working with local communities. Our guiding objective is to contribute, in a practical way, to restoring the balance and symmetry to the economic, social, spiritual and ecological welfare of individuals, communities and corporations. Why us and not a university, for example? Because this is driven by people – their needs and the issues that concern them – and not by funds.

The research aspect is important because without knowledge or facts, it is not easy to change things. There are a lot of people with opinions about all these issues, but opinions are not convincing if they are not supported. The Applied/Practical aspect is of enormous importance. This is not research for research's sake.

The Centre is unique in that it has grown from the ground up. It aims to articulate and disseminate ideas and approaches that contribute to this debate. It will work with corporations, organisations and institutions that are prepared to take the findings on board. Already, we have experienced the vital importance of this kind of applied research through a programme we have been involved in with University College, Dublin, and 160 family-farming people. The findings could have implications for 24,000 families who produce food, are responsible for the environment and connected to creation.

A number of leading figures from Irish society have agreed to act as Associate Members of the Centre. A Research Committee drawn from the worlds of academia, law, medicine, business and local communities has been established to oversee activities and research carried out by the Centre. A small staff has been put in place and initial funding has been committed by the ESB. A structure is now in place that will enable the work to be managed and carried out, and the findings applied. A number of areas have been identified. I should point out that these are issues that touch the lives of ordinary people – where they are. These are:

The Corporation and the Community
Constructing a response to the problems of globalisation can take many forms. One of the most effective may be the integration of corporations with local communities and the local environment. We are putting a framework in place to establish ways in which corporations can form links with families and communities.

The State of the Family in Ireland
The family in the past has been central to society. In a short space of time, we have moved from the extended family to the nuclear family to the single-parent family. What is happening to family? What implications do these changes have for society?

Voluntary Participation in Community Activity
How powerful a force is voluntarism? We have already commenced work on this issue. Without the voluntary movement, many services would disappear. There is a great spiritual power in this movement; people are sharing their time, energy and talents with others, improving the lot of their fellow men and women.

Local Resources and the Community
The concept of sustainability is a development concept that refers to the capacity of an area to self-generate. The concept is significant in that it is about combining economic success with a return to fundamentals such as roots, place, people and soul. A return to the people and the local resources is a key concept.

Community Itself – What is it? How Relevant is it?
Irish society is rooted in a strong sense of community. That sense of community is threatened by the perceived imbalance between the local and the global, the urban and the rural, among others. Valuing the local as a rich resource in its own right and rediscovering connections may be one of the greatest challenges facing us. We hope to carry out research and to carry out a number of community profiles. Efforts are being made to establish a sense of community that will respond to the challenge.

Spirituality and Values
Our society is searching for meaning. There is no doubt that the concepts of spirituality and community are emerging as the language of practical society. We have already begun work on the idea of people engaging with Christianity and taking responsibility for what it means to be Christian in practice. Christianity happened for most Irish people. Modernisation will challenge engagement with Christianity or ignore it.

Other
The social economy, education and sport are other issues that have been identified.

The emphasis in all of the above is on the local community. Our organisation has been working closely with local communities. We are very aware of the impact of the global culture and the need for balance, and these are some of the areas we have identified. A vital role for the Centre will be to ground research findings in real life. It will contract out some of the work and get involved directly in the rest. It will involve people at community, corporate, institution and university levels. It will identify and provide appropriate platforms for various debates, devising practical working programmes and consulting relevant parties. It will, of course, continue to run the annual conference and highlight some of the findings at these conferences.

We are happy with progress so far and I am very grateful for the commitment and support we have already got from individuals and institutions. We are particularly grateful to the ESB for adopting this as their millennium project. The ESB, as we know, touches, or more appropriately, lights up the lives of most people in this country. Our hope is that the Centre will make some contribution to doing the same.

UPDATE ON NETWORK OF VOLUNTARY GROUPS

Mary Redmond

I am really pleased to be here again today, almost a year to the day since I was with you in 1998. You may remember that last year I asked 'Is the social entrepreneur a new authority?' I described the community and voluntary sector as a potentially very important new authority in our millennium. Potentially rather than actually – it is infrastructurally unsound. It succeeds against all the odds because of the people by whose spirit and energy it is driven. The people are wonderful. The systems are not so great. The wheel of voluntarism is as yet unturned. Think how powerful it will be when it is turning, its spokes accommodating the rich diversity of the sector, its centre the distillation of the great energy that drives it, and of the even greater energy that it produces.

Last year I envisaged a cohesive sector as a 'wheel'. We all know that the wheel is one of the most important inventions of humankind. Its function is to transmit motion, so it is very powerful – not just process but motion. 'The Wheel' will transmit motion in the community and voluntary sector by bringing together communities of interest, 'the Spokes'.

At last year's inspirational conference there was a call to adventure and many of you generously came to Dublin the following week and endorsed and mandated The Wheel. Sr Thérèse spoke last year of her wish that seeds of hope would be sown as a result of the conference. I believe that they were sown by all of us together. I am very privileged to be back here today, to have the opportunity to tell you something of what has happened during the year.

The Wheel is spinning. We have had three major meetings, which were facilitated in a carefully thought out, creative way. Hundreds of people were brought together from as many diverse groups. They sought and were able to find commonalities. If diverse groups can do this, how much more so will the Spokes? The motion transmitted by

The Wheel takes place at round tables, where people meet equally. We believe in participative democracy. We describe these round-table meetings as equivalent to a legislative meeting. Each meeting is part of a journey, just as these conferences are.

During the last year the concept of The Wheel has been developing. It is not, I am glad to say, an organisation, it is not a federation, it will never be a national umbrella body or a funding agency. It is none of these things. I hope it will never be bogged down – here I speak against my own profession's regulations or by-laws. Of course, we have a limited company to receive money, because every organisation, every movement, must be accountable. The company is called *Rotha Teoranta*.

The concept of the Spokes developed during the year. A Spoke can be either temporary or permanent. It can relate to people from one or more areas of the community and voluntary sector. I might be involved in a Spoke on disability for example, but equally I might want to become involved with other groups who are dealing with women's issues, or with housing, or wherever disability is going to be relevant. There is a fluidity about the Spokes. Nobody is obliged to join a Spoke. But the Spoke is what brings together common issues. The work begins to result from that. A Spoke may or may not wish to have a voice. But a very important point that has emerged is that nobody or no Spoke may say 'We are speaking on behalf of The Wheel, we represent the community and voluntary sector'.

You might be interested to hear what some of the common issues are. Volunteers with project managers have been working on these throughout the year. They are education, training, communication and information technology. The primary issue that has come up in all of these is the need to select, share and store information. Anybody who is in business today will know that, no matter what you are doing, information is the key. Unfortunately for the community and voluntary sector, there is no one-stop shop where you can get information on educational courses, to take one example. The sector has got very little, probably no presence in the information society. It is a great tragedy that people are galloping ahead, companies are getting onto the Net, it is cost effective, and yet the community and voluntary sector is far behind.

Being in Ennis, I am speaking to a converted audience as regards the information society. I want to say more about what The Wheel has been doing in this regard. We have been testing cutting-edge technology. I invite you to go and look at our website, which is at www.wheel.ie. We have been looking at how best we can create a presence for the sector, how we can digitally connect the sector, not just organisations within the sector but the people who benefit from them and who work for them. Minister Dermot Ahern released one of his civil servants, one of his IT staff, to drive this project forward. During 1999, as we have been driving The Wheel forward, we have seen such a speed of change, shifting sands and goalposts going all over the place. The story that we are going to tell very shortly on 15 November at our next Harvest Meeting will be exciting. I will give you some flavour of what we will be telling you. On its own initiative, The Wheel has developed an e-mail and webmail system that can ramp to give an e-mail address to everybody in the community and voluntary sector. Today, the technology that we have developed with the engineers has a two-hundred-thousand-person capacity, but a capacity of several million will not be a problem. Just think, if there was a webmail system for all in the sector, how useful it would be in terms of adding value to our work, so that we could put first things first and concentrate on what is urgent. We are using chat-room software effectively, we have working discussion boards where people can start topics and contribute to various debates.

I mentioned earlier that we are founded on participative democracy. I think that in July we were the first large meeting to use the Internet to vote. You may have seen on the newspapers last week that there was a testing of electronic voting in the local by-election in Dublin. Well, we had electronic voting at all of our tables at our meeting in July. I can report for history that the first matter put to the vote of the community and voluntary sector at that meeting was 'Shall we have lunch?' One person said 'Maybe'. We will shortly have a new voting system which will be capable of having a dozen or more options.

One of our project briefs in this area of technology was to make using the Internet easy. So we have been using SmartCard technology. You have a magic little box, you put in a SmartCard, all the codes are on it, you plug it into your telephone line and away you go. The box is touch-sensitive. You open it up and there is the screen in front of you. You can press for Internet and press for e-mail. We are aware that this sort of SmartCard technology will provide many potential opportunities for other providers to piggyback their solutions onto these cards. The sector has got far more potential than it may realise. Disabled and deaf people as well as nominees of the National Parents Association are taking part in Wheel pilot studies. The Wheel technical office in Maynooth, the ISP Esat and the device company are all Irish. In less than a year, in just this one area, The Wheel has made a cyberleap for the community and voluntary sector. The sector has a presence that otherwise it would not have had. We have the beginning of the one-stop hub.

I have been speaking so far about tangible benefits, but just as important, I believe, are the intangible benefits that Wheel participants feel within and that flow from these meetings. The meetings have produced spontaneous sharing of wisdom and of experience. They have produced friendships. Perhaps most importantly, people come away feeling affirmed in the richness of life. I may be very involved in hospice or in parish care but if I go to a meeting of The Wheel I will meet people around the table who are involved in Irish language, theatre, disability, mental handicap, community and so on. The whole panoply of life. There is a sense of the richness of life of which we are so often unaware.

Last year we looked at the issue of the new millennium and we shared a dream about how life might be better. I would like to thank you for your support and for your trust last November. Now more than ever we need the courage to continue this journey.

I will end with a few lines from a poem called 'Kyrie', by David Gascoigne, which I have always appreciated:

> *Grant us extra ordinary grace*
> *O Spirit hidden in the dark in us*
> *and deep*
> *and bring to light the dream out of our sleep.*

3

CORPORATE RESPONSIBILITY TO COMMUNITIES

Stephen Covey

Dr Stephen Covey, co-founder and vice-chairman of Franklin Covey Company, the largest management and leadership development organisation in the world, addressed the conference, via video link, from Brigham Young University, Utah, a link made possible on the Irish side by the Ennis Information Age Town Project. Dr Covey was welcomed and introduced to the audience by session chairman, Kevin Kelly. Dr Covey responded:

> *I wish I were there with you in person. I lived in Ireland for many years and I love that country and the people. I admire your desire to deal with these issues that will powerfully affect your lives, your families, your communities and so forth, into the new millennium. I'm happy to participate with you and I look forward to our interaction in the question-and-answer period after this opening formal presentation.*

A while back I was in Sydney, Australia, watching a football game. They call it Australian rules football. I was looking at it through the lens of American football, which is gridiron football. I really could not make much sense of the whole thing, because it seemed to be a combination of that kind of football and soccer and other things I did not understand. I had to really work hard and depend particularly on the person next to me to explain what was happening, but I came to see it as a kind of metaphor for what is happening generally in the world. I think Stan Davis put it very succinctly when he said, 'When the infrastructure shifts, everything rumbles.' In other words, when we begin to experience the profound, constant and ongoing change, largely driven by the globalisation of technology, in the globalisation of markets, everything is affected by it. It's so easy to become a victim to it all and to lose a sense of control.

We remember as we go back in history. As we shifted from one infrastructure to another, everything changed. When we went from a hunting and gathering society to an agricultural society, almost 90 per cent of the people were profoundly altered in their lives. Everything changed. They were downsized. When we moved from the agricultural age into the industrial age the same thing happened and everything rumbled, as it were. Again as we move from the industrial age into the information age and intensive communication age, the same thing is happening, and I think we have yet to see the full impact. I go around to different audiences all over the world and ask them, 'How many of you are directly connected to some kind of global competition, where your competition is not local?' It is still a relatively small percentage of hands that go up. I ask them, 'In the next five to ten years do you believe that your organisation will be directly impacted by this global economy?' Usually about 50 to 60 per cent of hands go up. I ask them, 'Do you believe you will be indirectly impacted by the power that the global economy is going to have in raising the bar on standards everywhere?' Usually 70 to 80 per cent respond.

In my opinion it is going to happen faster and more profoundly than most of us even imagine. You are beginning to see an illustration of this on the Internet. I mean an 800 per cent increase in one year is staggering and it is, in my opinion, illustrative of the kind of world that we live in. It is not American football. It is a whole new game, and when I stopped there and watched that [Australian] football game I said, 'This is very much like what is going to happen. I am going to have to learn this. I am going to have to change myself and I will have to learn a new mindset that can deal with this. There has to be a skillset to deal with it effectively, and successfully. We all know the Aesop's fable about the goose and the golden egg, how this poor, impoverished farmer comes across this goose – it is his favourite goose. Under the goose he finds this golden egg and the farmer is temporarily thrilled. But then he thinks someone has tricked him in some way and throws it away. Then, on second thought, he decides to test it. He takes it to the assayer and it ends up being pure gold. Of course he is thrilled. He can hardly believe his good fortune. The next day he comes back and there is another one and the next day there is another one and another and they just keep coming and he becomes very wealthy, fabulously wealthy and overjoyed. He becomes also very impatient. He wants them all and he wants them now. In his greed and impatience, he cuts open the goose to get all the eggs. In so doing he kills the goose and, of course, there are no more golden eggs.

If you study the movement from the great infrastructural changes over the history of society, this happens constantly. People get into a victim state toward what is happening and they begin to respond to it. They are not intentional and conscious in the way they organise and manage their response. They are just victims to it and they do not know what to do. They all want to have the goose and the golden egg. They want to have balance in their lives. They do not want to neglect their families or to see community life and the life around traditional neighbourhood, the parish, the community and the family, deteriorate, because that is the goose. But the new reality has come upon them and it is very powerful and extremely seductive. It is an economic reality. Unless people take control of the situation and, in an intentional and conscious way, manage their response and manage their future, inevitably what will happen is that the goose will become sicker and sicker and eventually perhaps might even die.

I see this happening a great deal in my country. Sadly, the thing that got me into a lot of this material was a literature review that I did while I was working on my doctorate. It was on the success literature in my own country, going right back to its founding in 1776. It covered a two-hundred-year period, and it was fascinating to see what happened. How, little by little, the whole sense of the character ethic, as I call it, was gradually replaced by a personality ethic, by techniques, and by technologies. Little by little, the goose – the trust, the community, the strength in the family – started to suffer a horrendous loss, and a horrendous price was paid. It is being paid today and you can see it in many of the communities in my country. I also think there is a force operating to deal with that and to take a more conscientious approach, to rebuild and to strengthen and to feed the goose properly.

I also find, in my work with corporations, that they become so short-term focused that the short-term bottom line tends to dominate almost everything. It eventually ends up killing the goose, it kills the trust inside organisations. Just to illustrate, I frequently ask this question: 'How many of you honestly believe that the vast majority of the workforce in your organisations possess far more creativity, talent, intelligence, resourcefulness, ingenuity than their present jobs require or even allow them to use?'

It is a profound form of disempowerment. There is such energy and talent and resourcefulness that is not even allowed to be used. I then ask another question. This is a question that looks at the quality of the goose's life: 'What percentage of the time and energy in your organisations is spent on defensive and protective communication, in other words, in a personal conflict, in a departmental rivalry, operating on hidden agendas, reading the tea leaves – defensive forms of communication?' This could range from 25 to 50 per cent, or higher. What that illustrates is a low-trust culture, and when trust goes down, communication is negatively impacted. People are not open, and authentic and real and small weaknesses are exacerbated. People are always looking between the lines. You live in memo haven. Everyone worrying about their backsides is an illustration of a low-trust culture that often comes about because a short-term approach was taken to get golden eggs. And when trust goes down, eventually there are fewer and fewer eggs. One of the problems is that our information system is so focused on short term and there is so much attention given to the rewards attached to short term, that you think, why do I not go for it? But the net effect of it is, you kill the goose and the trust goes down inside the organisation.

Let me use a couple of figures to illustrate this. Figure 1 is of a tree showing the *character* and the personality ethic. This is a kind of summary of the literature review I did in my own country covering a period of over two hundred years. You will see a tree and there are two parts to the tree, the *character,* which is based on principles, and the *personality,* which is technology. That's congruent, you see – the tree comes of the roots, but what happened in my country is that, little by little, a separation, a truncation took place between *character* and *personality,* and that has created a tremendous amount of trust issues inside communities and inside organisations, which has hurt, in my

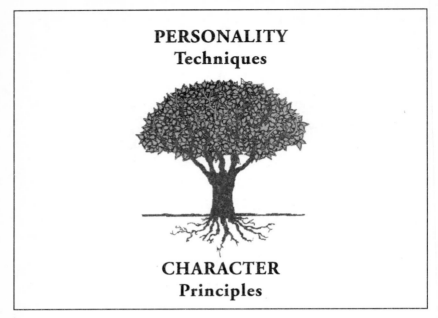

Figure 1

judgement, the balance of people's lives. Many people are trading that off in the name of economic success. In the short run, that does not work. I mean, it does work and it impresses people, but in the long run the hens come home to roost, and it is estimated that in my country 50 per cent of the marriages will end up in divorce and new marriages. Think what is happening to the children. You have gangs or surrogate families. People have such a need for belonging and acceptance. Young people do, and if they don't feel really intrinsically regarded and loved at home they will go where they can get that, even if criminality is the code of acceptance.

I mentioned that there is a growing awareness of what I am talking about. The other day I attended a large conference, put on by Fortune, for the Fortune 500. These are all of the top 500 organisations, and comprise what is called the Fortune 500. There were about two to three hundred CEOs there. They had a session on the question of how you are going to stay at the top of your craft over the next decade. What are you doing as the top leader of the organisation to stay at the top of your craft? Someone started talking about what they were doing in their corporation to deal with the kinds of problems I am talking about – in the community, in schools, the safety of the streets, what is happening to families – and that absolutely captured everyone's attention and interest. They started to share ideas with each other, such as adopting a school. Our corporation has adopted a school and we are resolved to work as a partner with that school, to help provide what they need. Sometimes it is just human capital. Sometimes it is real capital. Sometimes it is simply moral support and sometimes it involves encouraging our people to be very concerned about what is happening with their children at school. Someone would say, 'You know, we tried adopting a school, but it did not work. There was just such a strain and tension between the educators and the business people and no one really listened to each other.' 'This is what we did,' someone else said, 'because we had the same problem.' They chipped in and it became very authentic, very spontaneous. People were truly creative with each other and it was so consuming that it just went on and on and the Fortune people were wise enough to allow it to go on.

There was so much energy there, it totally eclipsed the other agenda and it went on and on for a much longer period of time than had been scheduled. People were really excited about it. They broke into small groups, sharing best practices. They were all concerned about what was happening to their communities. It was hard to attract people to communities that were not safe, to schools that did not have good solid cultures, that focused upon the growth and development of the children to become responsible citizens and to really master their own livelihood skills and so forth. It was a fascinating experience. I was overwhelmed myself to see the amount of energy. That's why, whenever I go around, I try to make myself available to help to do community work. I have ended up spending over one-third of my time and my speeches on a pro bono basis, because I am so convinced that we must do these things that build the family and build the community, for the safety of the streets and our children.

Inside our organisations we need to take a balanced score-card approach, so that we are not just looking at the financial bottom line, we are also looking at what's happening to our people and what is happening to their families. We need to think creatively through ways that will preserve the family, particularly when you have both parents working. If there are little children in the home, that makes it very difficult. In fact, if any of you have care-givers, I am sure that you want to be so careful, more careful than you would be in recruiting and selecting an employee, because they are, in a sense, influencing your greatest responsibility, your children. That is the ultimate goose of the future and that cannot be sacrificed on the altar of short-term economic prosperity and growth without terrible consequences in every direction.

People ask 'Is this really possible with all these forces that are descending upon us, the pressures, the stresses? Is it possible to keep this kind of balance, to keep wisdom?' Looking at the goose and the golden egg, my answer is absolutely, 'It is possible.' Not only is it possible, but you would achieve more in both areas. But it takes a conference like you are going through and the discussions that you inevitably have, and other things that nurture a conscious and intentional approach, to decide what it is we can do to get this balance between the goose and the golden egg, to preserve our values, our traditional way of life.

I know from my experience in Ireland that the thing I admired most was the authenticity, the genuineness of the people and the fact that relationships matter more than things. They were not just into efficiency, they were into what I would call effectiveness. That is, going for the results that really matter. This was so deeply inbred into the psyche and the intergenerational culture of this country that it was enormously attractive. Of course the physical environment was also enormously attractive but to have the human and the physical together made this one of the most lovely and beautiful experiences of my life. Sandra, my wife, and our children feel the same way. One of our children, Seán, was born in Ireland.

Now with this so called 'Celtic Tiger' and the tremendous energy that is happening and the new technologies and the global economy and the prosperity that many are experiencing, you are going to go through the same kinds of processes that my country has. I am sure you are, and you are trying to deal with the changes. Let me give you a few ideas as to what I have learned on how to deal effectively with them. I am going to look first at a diagram that represents some

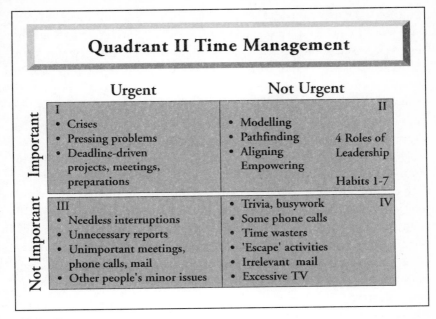

Figure 2

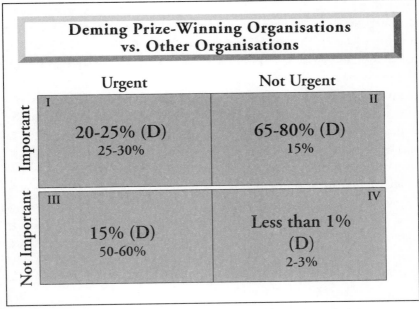

Figure 3

information we gathered on those great organisations in the world that have won the Deming Prize [see figure 2]. The Deming Prize is one of the most coveted and prestigious awards given. It is not just given for private organisations like corporations, but it is given for public ones as well. It is given on the basis of their performance against economic criteria and also against the 'goose' criteria – what is happening to the people, what is happening to the customers, what is happening to suppliers, to employees and to community. Because life is an eco-system, everything is related to everything else. I have just noticed from the data some very interesting things. There are four quadrants. The first quadrant is called 'Important and Urgent'. These are crises. The second quadrant is 'Important but not Urgent'. This is what I call the leadership quadrant. You are doing something today that is really not urgent. You could get this in other ways. You could do it at other times. It is not a crisis but it is important or you would not be here. Your time is very valuable. Look at quadrant three. 'It is Urgent but not Important.' These are the things that are on your desk. They are the phone-calls and most meetings. In fact, we have found that most report forms are never even read. Most meetings do not even need to be held. Many of them could be cut in half; they represent something that is pressing, like a deadline, but it is not truly important. Then quadrant four is 'Neither Important nor Urgent'. Keep looking at this for a moment. You can pretty well ignore quadrant one and four simply because they are 'washes' in comparing the Deming Prize-winning organisations with others. But look at the difference between two and three. The great organisations, the leaders, the executives, the managers, in those organisations are spending most of their time in quadrant two, and only about 15 per cent of their time in quadrant three. The other organisations studied are spending 50 to 60 per cent in quadrant three, and only 15 per cent in quadrant two. That is totally amazing. [See figure 3.]

That is the difference between a crisis management approach that defines urgency as the criteria of importance but, in fact, quadrant three is 'Very Urgent but not Important'. It can be neglected, as well as four. By attending to quadrant two, you begin to get a clear sense of what matters most. The problem with the organisations, the other organisations studied, is that there is no line between one and three.

We had to create it. Only by asking them questions did they come to realise that, yes, these urgent things are not important. The Deming Prize organisations had a line there. Even though they did not use this kind of chart, they knew what mattered most. They had paid the price in gaining and understanding what is truly important. This amazing data teaches that the problem is not the business of life and the profound changes. The problem is that we have become victims to it. We have not conscientiously decided what matters most in this new environment and enabled ourselves and organised ourselves to accomplish what matters most. Consequently the goose gets neglected and what is urgent and pressing gets attended to.

We have also done some surveys on what is holding back quality. We have found that the number one issue is low trust. We have done surveys on what is holding back empowerment. The number one issue deals with the misalignment of structures and systems in organisations that nurture trust. In other words, people say they value co-operation but in fact they reward competition, internally. They say they value the balance between short and long term but in fact they reward short term. The accounting system itself calls what you are experiencing today [attending the conference] an expense. It is not considered an investment. But if we buy a machine, that is called an investment that we can amortise over time. If you invest in people it is called an expense.

I just returned from visiting Egypt. What is Egypt trying to do? They are trying to continue to lead the Arab world into the new millennium and the new global economy. But they have a profoundly disempowered society, hierarchical, with an extremely profound caste system. Consequently they have co-dependency between the people at the top who are making all the important decisions and the rest who are wielding the screwdrivers and are passive and waiting until told. There is no empowerment. How are they possibly going to be what Rosabeth Moss Kanter calls the four imperatives of economic success in the new economy – focused, friendly, fast and flexible. If there is no empowerment in the people who are going to produce the quality, who are going to be interfacing with the customers, internal and external, it won't happen.

Training to them is a sideshow. It is not main tent. What is all this leadership talk that we are going through today? It is a sideshow. They can hardly wait to get back to the main camp where they get the real work done. But to Deming Prize-winning companies this is the main tent. It is not a sideshow. The decision regarding what matters most is main tent. You cannot make that from the top. You can't announce it. You can't rush it. With people, fast is slow and slow is fast. Have you ever tried to be efficient with your spouse on a tough issue? How did it go? Have you ever been efficient with a surly teenager on a tough issue? How did that go? Efficiency with people does not work, unless people buy into the same value system, the same overall purpose. Then efficiency is a value – but in the creation of that value system, in the creation of that criterion that governs every other decision, you cannot be efficient.

There has to be a deep buy-in from janitors, from people at the low end of the working scale, so that they co-mission with the criterion that matters most. Otherwise you get a polarised culture. Let me show you the two kinds of dilemmas that will come out of this polarised culture. The management dilemma is one. There is profound

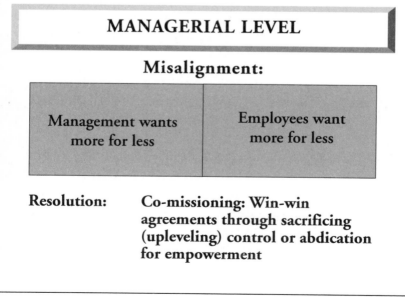

MANAGERIAL LEVEL

Misalignment:

Management wants more for less	Employees want more for less

Resolution: Co-missioning: Win-win agreements through sacrificing (upleveling) control or abdication for empowerment

Figure 4

misalignment, as you can see in figure 4. Management wants more for less. Employees want more for less. Management wants more productivity for less cost. Employees want more money for less time. That is misalignment. Why? Because there is no co-missioning taking place. Why? No leadership. Not the kind of leadership that shouts and announces and tries to psych people up, but the leadership that comes from deep trustworthiness in one's character, leadership that nurtures trust. The leadership that listens to people genuinely with the heart and the eyes, not pretending to listen, but really listening and being impacted by what they hear. The leadership that involves people sincerely, that deeply believes in the democratic concept that everyone has precious value and needs to be listened to and respected – that kind of leadership.

The net effect of the organisationally misaligned situation is that it causes the organisation itself to become misaligned with the marketplace business, and by business I mean generic business. Business is governed by the economic rules of the marketplace, but organisations are governed by the cultural rules of the workplace. If there is a low-trust culture, this profound misalignment will take place and this organisation or society will not be able to compete successfully in a global economy. When you are up against a raised standard of quality, lower cost, flexibility, speed to market, this takes a deep commitment from the people and the culture to make it happen. What are some of the things you can do then to conscientiously and intentionally take control of your own future?

I recommend that everyone develop a personal mission statement. Mission statements always start with the individual. Develop a deep sense of what your life is about and the values that you want to operate on. Listen to your conscience. Don't just ask what is it I want. Ask instead what is life asking of me. Your mission statement should include the totality of your life. Not just your worklife but all the significant roles of your life – your family, your community, your church, your friends, your different work assignments and stewardships. You have to deal with them all. Once you have inwardly decided what the important roles of your life are, in light of your value system and your mission, then you need to begin to organise yourself accordingly, setting up goals under each role, and you need to do it at least on a weekly basis, not on a daily basis. If you organise your life on a daily basis I guarantee you 'quadrant one thinking' will consume you. You will be into crisis management and you will be constantly intending to pay attention to things that matter most, like your family, community service, your help, your integrity – but little by little it can get eroded away, and the goose will begin to die.

Half the energy most people spend is on things that are not important but are urgent. I am going to neglect that; I am going to use that energy to focus on the leadership quadrant in deciding what truly matters most, involving people and helping them also to evolve the value system. To hold everyone accountable to it, including the top people, so that they are giving an accounting to their own people, to their culture, just as they require the people who report to them to give an accounting, so that no one is exempt from living by the values that the group has decided upon. That is what creates this hierarchical organisation, the caste system, that says people are different. The law applies to some but not to others.

An amazing thing happened in my country about six months ago. The whole country was mesmerised watching the television and literally watching the President of the United States being impeached in the House of Representatives, and the very next day, in the same exact place, in the same House, the President of the United States received twenty-eight standing ovations and most of them bipartisan. Why? Because values have become institutionalised, they may not be totally inculturated because you see prejudices and weaknesses. But they have become institutionalised, so that everyone is subject to the rule of law, including the President of the United States. Saddam Hussein promised his sons-in-law, during the Gulf War, that if they would return home from defecting, if they would come back they would be forgiven and given amnesty. That very day they returned they were both shot. Why? No institutional agency or moral authority.

When you have a society or an organisation or a family that really lays claim upon certain fundamental values and institutionalises those values, you're no longer that dependent upon the individual. People become increasingly independent, emotionally, mentally, economically and socially. Therefore, their own lives are more a function of their choices than a function of their circumstances. But if people are not intentional about these processes and deeply resolved to focus upon leadership, what happens is they become victims of circumstances and get tossed and turned about and driven by the urgency. Then they lose so many other important values that are still deep in their hearts, values that are precious, but have never been institutionalised. There is no formal system of double accountability, of what I call double bottom-line accounting, which means you study the financial side and you also study what is happening to all of the stake-holders. You can present the data in two pages, one for the financial, the golden eggs, and one for the goose. We do not have the time today to go into that but it is a very intriguing idea. It is called the balanced score-card and if we could get this institutionalised to where society with its tax system would respect it, it would reinforce it.

I have worked in countries that are working to do that. In fact in Egypt I recommended it. I was working with many of the top people on the business cabinet and other top leaders there. They nurtured the kinds of laws that not only encourage foreign investment, but encourage investing in people, seeing it as an investment rather than as an expense, so that there would be a deep respect given to all people at all levels of the organisation. That would be one factor among many others that would help empower the new workforce to be equal to the demands of the new economy.

Now, let me mention what I believe to be the four roles of this kind of leadership that occupies the essence of quadrant two. At the centre is modelling. What do you model? Trustworthiness – that's what nurtures trust. Pathfinding deals with your mission, your vision, your value system. Aligning deals with institutionalising that mission, that vision, that value system, that path. Those three together create trust in an environment and are the conditions for the fourth role, empowering. You will notice all of these words are verbs, modelling, pathfinding, aligning, empowering. Here you require constant attention day to day. I am not talking about management. I am talking about leadership. Making sure that the ladder is leaning against the right wall. No one wants to climb a wall and get to the top rung and then discover it is leaning against the wrong wall. You want to decide what that right wall is – that is pathfinding.

This can also be done on a community basis. In fact, my organisation is into about thirty different communities, where we are actually helping to train the people who are the leaders of schools, businesses, the city fathers and religious leaders, and joining together to come up with a common path, a common vision for the entire community, and then to make sure that there are laws and, hopefully, norms. Norms are the social part. Laws are the formal part. When norms are sufficient you do not need laws. When norms are insufficient you can't enforce laws. You have to work with both social norms and laws, to nurture the climate so that you have empowerment. By laws I mean the kind of laws that liberate people, the kind of laws that call what you are experiencing today an investment, not an expense. The kind of laws that preserve democracy for everybody, that value the worth of everybody.

Sometimes the norms of society are not there. There is bigotry. There is prejudice. There is inhumane treatment. There is child abuse. There is criminality. Sometimes people join groups whose norms focus upon those kinds of activities. What you need to work on is the overwhelming majority of the people and not to pay attention to extreme elements, so that you have a critical mass that is deeply focused on the basic values of that society. They are not going to be victimised by extreme elements or by small incidents that might get dramatised and exacerbated by the media because it attracts more attention and so forth. Steady as it goes. Roll with the punches. Smile a lot, but stay anchored, rooted and committed to that set of criteria that represents the path you want to take. That is your vision, and to have the discipline and the institutionalisation of that vision is the foundation that releases human potential.

Remember the question I asked at the beginning, where we acknowledged that the vast potential of people is still undeveloped. How can that be realised? Only when people have a common criterion and then they are given freedom with guidelines to do whatever it takes to accomplish that criterion, to accomplish that goal. You cannot really hold people responsible for the results if you supervise their methods. The moment you supervise methods you disempower people. You strangulate the culture. You polarise the culture. Trust goes down. The golden eggs become fewer. Why? Because the goose is sick and dying.

In summary, therefore, we are living in a new environment that is changing more profoundly and rapidly than almost any of us can possibly conceive of. It is truly staggering. This is going to require a mature, intentional, carefully thought-through leadership approach, so that you don't get victimised by all of these forces and end up killing the goose that lays the golden egg. This kind of leadership is not just a function of people at the top. It is a function of every person providing leadership at their level, so that they develop a personal mission statement (this, by the way, is one of the most significant things we ever did as a family) and then pay the price. Develop a family mission statement, where everyone is involved over time. So that you can preserve the feeling of 'we', and get away from this selfishness of 'me', where people begin to define pleasure and personal satisfaction as the object of their family life, instead of the kind of fulfilment that comes from a happy and strong family that enjoys each other, and also wants to contribute to the larger community. Another key point would be for executives of all organisations to think carefully through 'quadrant three' and neglect it. Neglect it! It is not important, but until there is a deep emotional buy-in to the criteria of what matters most, you won't be able to neglect it, because all these urgencies will tend to define importance, and then you will find, little by little, the trust will go down and the goose will get sick.

Well, why don't we open up? We can have some interaction. I think that it is in the interaction where much of the best learning, much of the best ideas come forth. It is just a tremendous pleasure to be with you and I want you to know that.

Questions and Answers
The following recounts the questions posed to Dr Covey and his responses to them.

Q. Stephen, how do you deal with cynicism and establish trust within established organisations where trust is not the norm?

R. I would say this. Cynicism is a symptom of a deep chronic problem. Let me give a recent experience that I had in a hospital. I had a friend who was the head of surgery and I asked if I would be able to visit some of his surgeries with him. He allowed me to do so. He also performed one himself. He was a cardiovascular surgeon. He replaced three arteries inside the chest cavity. I said to him, 'Is this man now clear?', and he said, 'Stephen, it is all the way through his system – feel.' He literally took my gloved, washed hand and guided me to different vessels inside the opened-up cavity. He said, 'Feel that.' It was brittle. You could sense the occlusion, the plaque material inside those arteries. He said, 'Fortunately this man is an exerciser and he has developed some supplementary circulation, because oxygen will force new arteries to form, to supply the nutrients for the muscles and so forth. But these three arteries, there is no supplementation, and if he had a blood-clot it could cause a heart attack or a stroke, so this is a chronic condition.' But there were no acute symptoms. This all came out of tests.

Now anytime you see cynicism, anytime you see internal dissention, that becomes very dysfunctional. Anytime you see disempowered people, the end effect of that is in the marketplace, so that you really lose market share. That is the acute symptom of a deeper chronic issue. Those 'four roles' that I identified really are the flip side of the deep chronic problems. Remember, at first I mentioned modelling trustworthiness. Well, at the centre of many organisations there is low trust, because people don't hold themselves to the same standards. Integrity is not the key and competence is not just integrity. It's to be competent and current. The flip side of pathfinding is that most organisations are not on the same song sheet, literally. If you want to test this for yourself tomorrow, go to your organisation and ask the first ten people you meet, 'What is the purpose of this organisation?' Write down what they say. Then ask them, 'What is the strategy, the main strategy, to accomplish that purpose?' Write down what they say. I guarantee you will be totally amazed at the differences being expressed. That is the criterion that drives everything else. Every other decision is governed by purpose and values and people are on the same song sheet. The flip side of alignment is profound misalignment, where people profess to believe in democracy but may practise autocracy inside their own organisations. I was with a large group of editors and newspaper publishers and I said, 'What is the purpose of your newspapers?' Basically, they answered, 'To keep democratic institutions honest and leaders honest.' I said, 'Do you really believe that?' 'Yes', they replied. 'How do you know if a person really believes something? Don't they try to live it, to practise it?' I asked. They said 'Yes'. I said, 'How many of you, in your own newspapers, have this function inside?' I have studied the trust levels inside those newspapers and they were very low. 'How many of you have that same trust function, I mean that function of providing to society, inside your own organisation?' Only about 5 per cent did. So the alignment issue is very important. Then you get empowerment. The disempowerment is the fruit. It is the acute manifestation of these deeper chronic problems. That is why a conference such as yours is such a healthy thing. To stand back and to say 'What is happening? We can take control of this. We don't have to become a victim of it.'

Q. I would like to know how your ideas can be used to promote social justice and equality. That is, to promote those ideas in society as a whole rather than just in families and organisations.

R. I will use a diagram to help my answer to this question [see figure 5]. You will notice on this diagram that there is a very large circle of concern. Notice inside the larger circle of concern is a smaller circle, called the circle of influence. You'll notice what your job is. Your job is partly inside that circle of influence and largely outside of it and inside your circle of concern. Now how do you work to bring about social equality and justice in society? The key is to give your full energies to your circle of influence, not your circle of concern. Of course you are concerned, but the moment you focus upon the circle of influence it will become larger.

Look at what Ghandi did. Ghandi, when he left South Africa with international notoriety, went back to India. The political leaders in New Delhi and Bombay were jealous of his tremendous moral authority. They were thrilled when he went into obscurity for many years. What was he doing? He was building relationships with people inside his circle of influence. He was deepening his convictions about social justice and equality and independence from Great Britain. He was getting to know the soul of India. Little by little, ten people would follow him, then fifty, a hundred, a thousand, ten thousand, and then

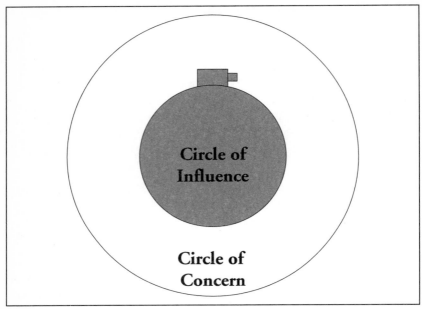

Figure 5

all of a sudden, one day, the telegram came into New Delhi and said he was coming. The political leaders, thinking Ghandi was obscure, said, 'Who is he?' Five hundred thousand people showed up at the train station. He was a phenomenon and he never was elected. He was a person of such moral authority. He worked inside a circle of influence until his circle of influence became larger and larger to where he would fast and heal religious division. He would fast and stop the killing of the British soldiers because his strategy was non-violence and the use of moral authority. The main problem that many people have is they get their minds and hearts focused on the weaknesses outside the circle of influence and it literally causes their internal circle to get smaller, not larger, because they have so much negative energy in them. They attract other people that massage their hearts, but other people feel they are a single-issue person and they stop listening to them. The key is always to work inside the circle of influence. There is one more symbol [on the slide] you will notice. It is a little rudder at the top of the circle of influence, and at the side of that rudder is another rudder called a trim tab. When you move the trim tab the small surface moves the larger surface. Ghandi was a trim tabber for many years. This takes patience.

So therefore, I would say, start with yourself. Are you a person who deeply believes in social justice, equality? Then your family. It is the child who tests you the most who is the key to family culture. Can you show unconditional love to that child, so that the others will know that they too are valued intrinsically? Then your organisation. Can you strive to get social justice and equality in your own organisation, in your own circle of influence, then your neighbourhood, then your community and your Church and the society as a whole? I am sure you can see the point I am trying to make. From my experience, this is the only approach to bringing about those precious values that you have identified. It is an inside-out approach, not outside-in. You can't be sitting here and wishing that the people who really need this were here.

Q. Why is there such huge imbalance between the concern that is expressed and the actual support that is given to services to strengthen the family? This concern seems to be ongoing but it is not followed up with resources.

R. That is a marvellous question. I think there is a great deal of imbalance while a great deal of lip-service is paid to balance, personally and organisationally. That is why I give such focus and energy to taking an intentional, conscious approach to developing a mission statement and to make sure that it is not lip-service to use that criteria to drive the alignment of structure in systems to serve that balance value.

That's where the real rub is. It really is. Those are the sacred cows. Those are the structures and systems that are often nurturing imbalance when in fact the mission statement professes balance. It is this hypocrisy we are all concerned with. We must start again in our circle of influence, to make sure in our own personal lives that we model this kind of balance. Then in our relationships with others and as employers we must respect the importance of balance with our own employees so that they know how important family is to us and to them. Both family and marriage, because the highest responsibility we will ever have on this earth is parenting and the greatest thing you will ever do for your children is to treat their mother or their father with respect. That modelling does more than anything else. Just treat them with respect, kindness and love, because they are bone of their bone and flesh of their flesh. By modelling it and creating a norm around this and then trying to nurture this, we must institutionalise it. It is the institutionalisation of the value that keeps it from being a lip-service. No one on their deathbed ever wished they spent 'more time at the office'.

Q. I was wondering if you agree that we need to extend your double bottom line to a triple bottom line, which also includes biological resources, as well as the economics and the people side of things, because ultimately we are biological beings?

R. Yes, I would agree with that, but the way I defined the double bottom line included the physical ecological side, as well as the social ecological side, so it is more a matter of definition.

Q. Do you think that profit-sharing has a place in the new organisation of the future as you envisage it?

R. Yes I do. I think those people who produce the wealth should share in it and one of the reasons why this does not happen is because of what I call a scarcity mentality. That means you see life like a piece of pie, so if someone gets a hunk of it, that means that others get less and that means you get less. This is one of the reasons why sometimes you see even loved ones not being genuinely happy for the success of their siblings and other loved ones. They might say they are happy, giving lip-service, but inwardly they are eating their hearts out. Much of our culture so focuses upon the concept of scarcity. We have a single career path in most organisations, not a double or triple. We have normal distribution curves and forced-ranking systems behind the compensation system in most organisations. That nurtures scarcity. When you get people with scarcity, if they share a profit they feel like they have less. The opposite takes place. It creates a synergy so that you have a cornucopia of something that gets larger and larger and larger.

It isn't where $1 + 1 = 2$. It is where $1 + 1 = 3$ or 5 or 10. There are many very powerful illustrations of this. You see, people think they are making a trade-off. If they try to get the balance in life they won't do as well in business. They will do better. People think that they are making a trade-off: if they share some profit they will have less. They will have more. Unless they have a scarcity mentality and they don't have integrity around these principles and they give lip-service to them, then I think scarcity becomes a self-fulfilling prophecy.

Q. Much of our conditioning, people choose to believe, is based around the fact that we are so influenced by the Famine and the British oppressing the Irish. Can we choose to liberate ourselves from this scarcity mentality that seems to be enshrined there because of our conditioning?

R. Let me use a diagram to help me in my answer, please [see figure 6]. In this diagram there are two models. The one at the top 'Stimulus – Response' has a space in the centre. The one at the bottom has no space between 'Stimulus' and 'Response'. The question deals with 'Are we a product of our past and of our conditioning and of the present

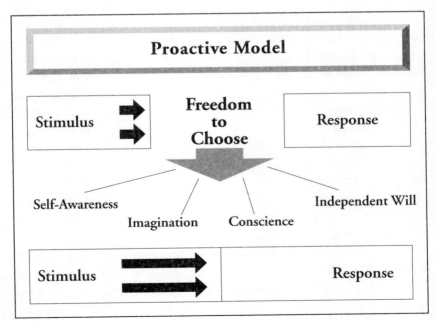

Figure 6

circumstances?' If the answer to that is yes, then the lower model applies and we become reactive. Animals are reactive. The upper model is the human model. We are not, I suggest, a product of our past. Of course it influences us profoundly but it does not determine us. If there is any space at all between stimulus and response, we have the power to choose our response, and the space becomes larger and larger the more we exercise that power. The key is to own that space. People possess human gifts, human endowments that animals do not have, and animals possess gifts and endowments that we don't have, but right now I am focusing upon these four that we have as human beings. We have self-awareness, which means, let's say, I was raised and conditioned in a family where love was given conditionally. I was abused and neglected but I am aware of that. I also have my imagination. I can see a different future in the way I raise my children. I have a moral sense called conscience that says abuse is wrong and giving unconditional love is right. I also have the power of independent will. Then I can act upon the other three. Now, it might be very hard for me, because this cultural psyche, the social and biological conditioning has been very, very strong, but I can reinvent myself. This is the reason for your conference. That you can consciously take control of the direction of your lives, of your organisations, and help influence your entire society. You are using these four unique gifts and endowments. We are not a product even of our biology. I might have a pre-disposition towards diabetes, because of my DNA genes, but I can choose my response to that awareness. Use my imagination, my conscience, my sense, that I have a responsibility to have a healthy life and to live a long life, for the sake of my children and grandchildren and for contribution to society, and also I have my power of will and I will never get diabetes. Why? You choose a regiment, a lifestyle. I admit there are some very, very aggressive strong biological forces that you can only choose your response to. You cannot necessarily change them.

I also admit there are mental diseases that sometimes keep us from having this space between stimulus and response. But in my judgement the overwhelming majority of people have that space and need to own it and not feel like they're a victim of their culture, their biology or psychic conditioning as a child. I am not a determinist.

Q. I'm sorry to inject some negativity into the debate. It seems to me that the society we are living in is actually no longer acknowledging the importance of the institutions on which your thesis seems to rely. A large number of people are choosing lifestyles that don't have traditional configurations of the family. Many of us have decided for whatever reason to abandon traditional religious beliefs but are still hungering for spiritual fulfilment. Most of all, organisations are heavily influenced by business values and driven by the short-term profit consideration. Could you just give it one more thrust so that I can respond to the other side of the feelings I am having, which are stimulus and excitement?

R. First of all, let me say, you do not inject negative energy. Energy comes from differences and from respect for those differences. This is what creates the synergy. Otherwise we clone people and you call it sameness because unity it isn't. True unity comes from synergy. That is where differences are expressed; you create something new, like a father and a mother creating a child. That is synergy. It came from the valuing of differences. I would also say that when I talk about the word 'organisation', I believe that the primary organisation is the family. I am not going to define for other people how that should be defined or configured. I am merely going to say that it is the nurturance of the children that is the supreme value, so that they grow up to be healthy, strong, contributing citizens, so that they themselves can carry on these traditional values of family and of community and of faith, as well as preserving the economic stability and prosperity of their society. Therefore, I take the broad view of organisation and I see the individual, the family, the neighbourhood and the community, before I see the workplace. I see that as the goose that lays the golden eggs in the workplace, that keeps the streets safe.

Q. I find it hard to imagine myself as a drop of water making an indentation in a rock. Can one person make a difference?

R. With regard to this idea of one more drop on the rock in trying to make a change, do you know any other way but to work inside your circle of influence? Think about it. Is there any other way? If you tried to work outside your circle of influence, by definition you have no influence. But if you work outside your job and inside your circle of influence, and your circle of influence is large, you can enlarge the circle of influence for other people. The trim tab is a very small rudder but it turns the big one.

The small drop may attract a whole rush of water from other people who identify with those values and there can be a powerful indentation into that stone. I don't know any other way myself. If you study all the great figures of history who have made a difference, you will find that basically their vision came from their personal moral authority, until gradually they began to influence the wider culture and it became institutionalised. I was with Mrs Sadat. She was at an international symposium and I asked her about her husband, Anwar Sadat, and his trip to the Kenesset in Jerusalem, which eventually brought about the Camp David Accord. I asked, 'What was it like living with this man?' She said, 'I was amazed when he took that bold peace initiative.' She confronted him and said, 'How can you possibly do this and betray all of what you have said to your people, that you would never shake the hand of an Israeli as long as they occupy one inch of Arab soil?' And he said, 'Because it is right. You cannot think independently in an interdependent world.' She said, 'You will lose the support of the Arab world.' He said, 'Perhaps, but I hope not.' 'You will lose the Presidency of Egypt.' 'I hope that will not happen, but it might.' 'You will lose your life.' He said, in response, 'My life will not be one minute longer or one minute shorter than it is ordained to be.' That was his personal faith. She embraced him and said, 'You are the greatest man I have ever known.' I asked, 'What was it like when he came back the next day?' She said, 'Normally it takes thirty minutes to get to our home. It took us three and half hours.' Why? The streets were lined with hundreds of thousands of people, cheering. The same people who were cheering the opposite message the previous week. There is a deep internal sense of right and wrong that is universal, timeless and self-evident. Such are the kinds of values we are talking about today – respect, diversity, integrity, service, social justice, equality and so forth. I am a great believer that however large your trim tab is, use it and let that be the source of your influence and get out of negative energy where you decry many, many people or institutions from afar.

Q. Organisations that are represented here, what can they specifically do tomorrow to start this new process?

R. First, I would rebuild one broken relationship that you care a lot about. I am very serious about that, because we all have some relationships that are perhaps not as strong as we would like. They may be broken or breaking or in neutral. The process of rebuilding that one will impact on you and that is the first and most fundamental step. Change yourself. Second, take what you have learned at this conference and teach it and share it with other people, not to shape them up, but simply to tell them what you have learned about yourself. Third, get feedback on your own leadership from people you work with and around. A good way to do this – and it can be done at no cost and give you about 80 to 90 per cent as good a feedback as you get from sophisticated sociological instruments – is just to use some kind of e-mail or anonymous form. It has to be anonymous. That is very important. Go to about ten or fifteen people. Get a note and just say 'I want to be more effective. I want to have more balance. I want to preserve the values of our society, of our community, of our family, of this company and so forth. Would you give me some feedback on my leadership under these three words:

- Continue
- Stop
- Start

"Continue! Would you like to see me continue?" "Stop! What is unhelpful and inhibiting and frustrating to you that you want me to stop?" "Start! What would you suggest I start doing?" '

You will be amazed with the feedback that comes. Express appreciation to those people and tell them you will do it again in six months. If the trust relationship is good enough then the normal day-to-day human interaction will give you this kind of feedback, and if you do this on a consistent basis it keeps you humble, open and teachable, and real and sincere. You are working on yourself. The fourth thing I would do is write a personal mission statement. Fifth, after I teach this and get this feedback and have a sense of my own values system, I would then involve other people in the kind of discussions that we are carrying on here, so that little by little you are a trim tab, influencing the larger rudder. This is an inside-out approach. It is not dramatic. It is not media-worthy. It is quiet but it works. You study Mandela. After twenty-seven years in prison, he comes out, comes to his own inauguration. He had paid such a price to win the private victory inside and he was so full of forgiveness and reconciliation that in the seats of honour he had his loved ones and his jailers. Then he brought in the ANC choir to sing the Afrikaaner anthem and the Afrikaaner choir to sing the ANC anthem. Then he appointed one hundred peace committees, primarily black women whom I helped train to some degree, to identify and defuse the hot issues.

Q. Stephen, is it Utopia when the personal mission statement is a reflection of the company mission statement and isn't just a wonderful piece of copywriting on a wall? Is that Utopia, when the two actually merge?

R. Yes. This is called co-missioning. You co-mingle the four basic needs of all people with the four basic needs of all organisations. The first one is an economic need. You have to live. The next one is the social need to have relationships, to love. The third one is the mental need to constantly learn to grow and develop. The fourth one is the spiritual need to have a sense of meaning and to have integrity towards the principles and the ultimate source of those principles that I, and most of us, believe is God. These are the four needs of our people.

Now I will show you the four needs of our organisations – the same ones. The organisation, economically, has to live; it has to have a bottom line. The wages of capital are profits. If profits aren't there, capital will go elsewhere. If people are not paid their wages they will go elsewhere. People have to live; the organisation has to live. The organisation has to have trust in it. Respect, kindness, how people are treated – love. The organisation has to adapt and learn, grow and develop. It has to learn in order to accommodate the new realities of the new economic world. The organisation has to have value to society in order to leave a legacy. It has to contribute and it has to have integrity. Co-missioning is a process of human interaction, the authentic empathic listening again. Empathic listening means you listen within the other's frame of reference and then you courageously express how you see it. The four needs of the individual and the four needs of the organisation overlap.

Then you have co-missioning; you have what the question called Utopia. Admittedly Utopia may not be achievable, but you are working toward it. You want as much co-missioning as you can possibly have. That creates a fire within, it creates internal motivation and you don't need to carrot and stick people, the great jackass theory of human motivation, where you have the carrot in front of them and the stick behind them. Instead, they can be motivated by these other four forces.

As part of the training that we provide, we show a short video presentation on these four needs. The core message of this presentation is that the basic needs of people can be summarised by their desire to live, to love, to learn and to leave a legacy.

Q. How much do you think education in the formal sense can contribute to the formation of 'goose-carers', people who will care well for the goose, and how, broadly speaking, might it do so?

R. I believe that, next to the home and family, education is the most significant institution to care for the goose. Where there is failure at the home and family level, I think it devolves on educators, primarily, to become, in a sense, surrogate parents and models to these children, so that the goose grows up healthy and strong. I totally feel aligned with your commitments and your value system.

Q. In the movement from character ethic to personality ethic, I just wondered, Stephen, do you think that positive thinking is enough? Is it enough or is it chicken soup ultimately?

R. Well, I believe that positive thinking is an important part but I do not think it is enough. You can put it this way. It is necessary but insufficient. You remember the four unique endowments – self-awareness, imagination, conscience and independent will – well, I would put positive thinking somewhere in the area of imagination.

But I would say that you need deep self-awareness, conscience and independent will and you also need to apply those same endowments collectively at the family, the business, the community levels, so that there is a collective will, a social will. So that there is a collective sense of conscience. So that there is a collective awareness of what is happening in today's world – the excitement of it, the possibilities of it, the dangers and the threats as well. So that there is a collective sense of vision, of imagination, that we can make significant moves. I think that Ireland is in a tremendous position internationally to do that, because you have so much, and, relatively speaking, I think it is undiscovered.

Q. Do you think that organisations should be challenged to spend two and a half hours a week or an hour a week in the community, getting in touch with the community at grass-roots level and making this part of their strategy?

R. Yes. I think that organisations should definitely be encouraging their people to be involved in community efforts and also to help lubricate the processes to make that possible, so that it creates some flex-time, some empathic awareness of where there are special needs and situations. I really do believe that we should all give at least a tithing of our time in community service and that organisations and families should do that. The social problems are accumulating. The social costs are enormous. I am convinced that if all of the stable, functional families were to build into their own family's mission statement the adoption, psychological adoption, of another family that is seriously at risk, or a child that is at risk, it would solve 90 per cent of the social problems of today. General Colin Powell just presented at our symposium the other day. He is heading up what is called 'America's Promise', to try to bring five things to the fifteen million children in America that are seriously at risk – inoculations when they are born, a safe place to go after school, the development of a marketable skill, and, most importantly, a caring mentor or adult, and then an opportunity to serve, to give back. If you were to get families who are healthy and functional to adopt psychologically another family and care for the children – or if they don't have that kind of a family, to reach out and psychologically adopt children that are seriously at risk – automatically those five things would be provided. Not automatically. Of course it would take real, serious attention but of course you would want to do these five things. That family would. Our family has adopted a family that is blended, coming from very difficult backgrounds – divorces and so forth. My wife has adopted scores of children who were friends of my own children, in their athletic clubs, but don't have parents that nurture them, and she has nurtured them. This thing works, if we could get everyone to make a commitment of at least a tithing of their time – and I definitely feel that corporations and so forth should encourage that kind of thing.

Q. What are the elements of a personal mission statement?

R. I will tell you a good way to do it. Imagine your funeral. Write four speeches that you would like to have given at your funeral. One from your loved ones, one from your friends, one from your work, your profession, and one from the community, the church and so forth. Really think carefully what you would like to have them say about you. Or a very simple alternative way to do this is just to write the epitaph you'd like to have on your tombstone. That forces you to think 'What is my life really about?' Second, think of each one of the important roles of your life – your family, your work, community, social, church and so forth. Now, what would you really like to be contributing in each of those roles? What kind of a person would you like to be? Are you a person that is focused on service and contribution or just me and mine? Are you a person that really wants to make a difference to society, like the people who are at your own conference? Obviously! Look at the spirit of what you are about. Sandra and I have done this on our own family mission statement. We envision our fiftieth wedding anniversary. We see the children, the grandchildren, the great grandchildren. We see it, we describe it, we envision it. Our kids do the same thing – we have so many children now – they all have family mission statements.

This is hard work. You have to think reflectively. You have to be very honest with yourself. It is so easy to come up with a lot of purple phrases, that you are giving a little lip-service to. You have to ask 'Am I really prepared to pay the price to do that?' Don't rush this mission statement. Take weeks, if not months to develop it. Mine took years. As it gets so seated inside you, it will govern the whole way you see life, and the way you try to serve others.

A VIEW FROM THE CHAIR

KEVIN KELLY

The scene was set. One sensed the anticipation from the 'capacity crowd'. One of the world's most influential speakers, Dr Stephen Covey's time had come. His message was simple yet elegant, concise yet complicated: 'To love, to learn, to live, to leave a legacy.' Having read his book before we 'E-met' and having listened to his contribution, these were the words that vibrated with my soul:

> Love – our search for love is a daily process, maybe our journey could be short-circuited by tuning into the Source;
> Learn – our appetite for learning about life should never be diminished, After all, life is a journey, not a destination;
> Live – living life today, remember here today, gone tomorrow, live life now;
> Leaving a legacy – I have unconditional faith that we all possess some talents that if used for the good of all can lead us towards a life of magic and adventure.

An elegant message that one should stick on one's desk at work, on the kitchen door, even imprint it on one's psyche. Have no doubt it will open the door in your life.

It was an honour to chair the session, even if I recognise that it wasn't my preordained role in life. The speakers throughout the two days impressed me not just for their wisdom, but also for their sincerity and their genuineness. I pray that genuineness and honesty will become currency in the world – life would be a lot simpler if they were. So where to from here?

Action
Harry Bohan rightfully urged people to take action, to engage in the process. His ambitions far exceeded the creation of another 'talk shop'.

This to me is the challenge. So many leave seminars with a buzz. Unfortunately, very soon this starts to dissipate and intentions of integrating ideas that resonated from seminars become a distant dream. But I can guarantee you one thing from my years in training: if you were to integrate only one idea from a seminar it could change your life forever. Why? Because life is not about taking significant action, it is about doing *anything*. The minute you engage you move to the next level.

Become aware

Remember that for those involved in this fascinating journey called life, you don't need to wait for the next seminar for new lessons; teachers are everywhere. Your next lesson could come in your local coffee shop. Only the ego stops you from believing that everyone can be your teacher. So the message is simple – trust with your heart, engage and watch your life become one of magic and adventure.

4

IRELAND: THE CHALLENGES OF SUCCESS

Tom Collins

In this paper I propose to explore a few ideas on the challenges facing Ireland as we move into the new millennium. I want to focus especially on the notion of change in Ireland, and on the theme of how, having resolved so many problems in the last few years, we are now finding that when we solve one problem, we merely move on to another one. This phenomenon of having to turn our attention from problems that we have become accustomed to trying to solve, to problems that we have no experience of trying to solve, raises interesting challenges.

I also want to explore the notion of generational change. Ireland, since the Famine, has been characterised by deep generational shifts in direction resulting in fairly fundamental upheavals, whereby the trajectory of the preceding generation is turned on its head, and a new trajectory emerges. I propose to look at the generational challenge confronting this generation and how that is being articulated in the national consciousness. I particularly want to look at two themes in this context, those of democracy and development.

I will begin on the theme of democracy by suggesting that there are two key forces driving the redefinition of democracy in modern Ireland. One is the experience of betrayal and the other is the process of globalisation. The concept of betrayal, particularly in relation to personal, intergenerational responsibility, is widely explored in the literature of modern Ireland, but perhaps nowhere more poignantly than in the poem of that name by Michael D. Higgins:

> *This man is seriously ill,*
> *The doctor had said a week before,*
> *Calling for a wheelchair.*

It was
After they rang me
To come down
And persuade you
To go in
Condemned to remember your eyes
As they met mine in that moment
Before they wheeled you away.
It was one of my final tasks
To persuade you to go in,
A Judas chosen not by Apostles, but by others, more broken.

. . . .

I look at your photo now,
Taken in the beginning of bad days,
With your surviving mates
In Limerick.
Your face haunts me as do these memories;
And all these things have been scraped
In my heart,
And I can never hope to forget
What was, after all,
A betrayal.[1]

This poem explores the theme of a parent's generation being betrayed by the child's generation; the older generation being betrayed by the younger one. In his book *Inventing Ireland*, Kiberd[2] draws attention to how, when a country is in transition, the younger generation turns its back on its parents and, in particular, how sons discard their fathers. The image of the failed father is a recurring one in twentieth-century Irish literature. The male characters in O'Casey's plays, for example, are typically drunken, garrulous and generally useless, being carried through life by valiant women. In *The Playboy of the Western World*, Christy Mahon needs to murder his father twice before he can walk with him in a degree of harmony. It is probably to be expected that this rejection would be accompanied by ambivalent emotions; the exhilaration of emancipation constrained by guilt.

Betrayal in contemporary Ireland is of a different kind. It is a betrayal of a younger generation by an older generation. This is a new experience. The many scandals that have plagued modern Ireland with regularity in recent years are effectively the betrayal of the present generation by the preceding generation. They pose a new challenge to the nature of democracy at a number of levels. Current scandals call attention to the civic nature of morality. The sense of betrayal that so many are currently experiencing arises from the belief that we have been sinned against by those in whom we had invested an expectation to behave morally. This poses a wider and more fundamental challenge to a society that must come to terms with a history of having invested faith in unworthy places. It isn't enough to seek retribution or atonement from the perpetrators; we must also as a society learn and develop from those events in terms of how we relate to authority and leadership.

In the light of this experience, the path of reconstruction as a society must begin with unbelief rather than belief. This is the challenge of scepticism rather than the challenge of cynicism. Cynicism, as Stephen Covey pointed out, is an entirely destructive preoccupation. Scepticism is a healthy negativity which requires that trust be earned rather than conferred. It looks to new processes of legitimisation that subject those in authority to a continuous test to show they are worthy of such authority. One of the common features of many of the recent scandals in Ireland is the fact that those who perpetrated them were in positions of power but were subject to few, if any, checks on their behaviour. While we must disapprove of the corruption that inevitably accompanies power without accountability, we should not be surprised by it. We should learn rather that structures that were entrusted with the responsibility of ensuring accountability clearly failed to do so through a combination of generalised silence, supine submission and tacit compliance. And we should ensure that this cannot be repeated.

This is not an entirely negative starting-out position. Psychologists such as Freud and Erikson saw the life-cycle as a series of progressive learning challenges. They asserted that each learning challenge, if negotiated successfully, allowed one to move on to a new stage of maturation, to a new energy towards growth and the development of wisdom. But they would also have said that it is sometimes possible only to revisit an earlier stage of one's life from the current stage. One can not revisit it while one is in it. This is surely the great value of history or at least of telling one's history, in that in telling it one gets freedom from it. This may be the ultimate purpose of the current tribunals and examinations; they are a recognition that society must confront its past before it can mature from it.

The foundation of the Irish State – designed to herald in democracy – really replaced one overlord with another one. The clericalised Roman Catholic Church, which attained pre-eminence as well as prominence on the foundation of the State, was a much more astute overlord in many ways than the colonial State that had preceded it. It spoke the language of the people. It recruited its leaders from amongst them and it positioned itself strategically at all of the key defining moments of life – at birth, at the age of reason, at adolescence, at marriage, at family formation, and at death. So life, even at its most private level, was orchestrated in a comprehensive, all-embracing and totally diligent way.

The religious process in Ireland within the Roman Catholic tradition was a process less of searching than of compliance. It was less disposed towards exploration than towards adherence. To search or explore was almost treasonable. Irish theology was much less concerned with the search for truth than with its transmission. Religious maturity became equated with ritualistic compliance. The folk memory in Ireland overflows with recollections of the clash between this form of compliance on the one hand and the daily lived experiences of the people on the other. It is important to note that this model of Church was an imposed model. It was not a native or indigenous model, nor indeed has it been of a very long vintage. David Roth, Bishop of Ossory in the early seventeenth century, took the view that 'Catholicism should eliminate barbarous customs, abolish bestial rights, and convert the detestable intercourse of savages into polite manners and a case for maintaining the Commonwealth'. Such a generalised, institutional adherence did not emerge from the ground up, but was imposed in much the same way as many of our other colonial impositions.

We are now in a process of moving out of this phase in our history. We are moving – if the numbers of those attending Mass or involved in seminaries, etc., are anything to go by – into a post-clericalised period in modern Irish history. We have had three generations of post-colonialism and we now perhaps have the first generation of post-clericalism. What will that mean for finding democracy? What will it mean for challenging our understanding of authority as something vested in somebody who is super-ordinate to myself? How can we be sure that the rapid erosion of one structure heretofore held largely unaccountable will not simply be replaced by others?

Globalisation

Globalisation as a process is now central to the emerging nature of democracy. A view of globalisation as the compression of time and space inevitably blurs distinctions between local and global and introduces global competition into what were heretofore largely local allegiances. Giddens[3] talks about the idea of 'generative politics'. This involves two main preoccupations. Firstly, it involves what he terms 'the interrogation of tradition', i.e., a qualified, conscious acceptance of tradition as opposed to an unqualified, habitual acceptance; a shift from prescribed certainties to negotiated conditionalities. The interrogation of tradition leads to a new form of relationship to the past, which, rather than leaving us with a sense of being disabled, allows us to rework it in exciting and new ways. In Ireland, the continuously evolving nature of 'traditional' Irish music is one example of this process. Here, in a process begun with composers such as Seán Ó Ríada and continued by others such as Mícheál Ó Súilleabháin, complemented by wide-ranging experimentation in the performing area by groups such as The Chieftains, the music inheritance of previous generations is being continuously recreated and enriched.

The interrogation of tradition also leads to new arrangements in society. This is what he calls 'the changing basis for solidarity'. Instead of being part of something because one was born into it, one is part of something because one selects into it. Relationships then are a matter of choice rather than legacy. This leads to a new understanding of individual autonomy, on the one hand, and the individual's relationship to the group, on the other. The basis of this is what Giddens calls 'active trust', i.e., trust that is earned rather than conferred. It is active in that it is constantly monitored and constantly checked out.

The concept of 'active trust' underpins new notions of governance. In particular, it signals a shift from a democracy of a purely representative nature to one that also embraces a participatory dimension. It stresses the notion of active citizenship as opposed to merely informed citizenship; and, ideally, it transforms the individual's relationship to the State from one of client-based passivity to one of partner-based agency.

The Development Challenge

Having looked at the changing nature of democracy in Ireland, I now propose to look briefly at the nature of development. It is becoming increasingly clear now that the analyses, priorities and mechanisms that have, at least for the present, succeeded in solving our growth promotion objectives are not appropriate to meeting the challenge of growth management.

Essentially, we have no history to guide us in how to handle the next ten years. We don't even have a language for it. Much of the language that we still use is part of a language of a past that has little relevance to the future. It's the language, for instance, of peripherality, or the language of isolation. The emergence of cyberspace means that with the necessary telecommunications infrastructure, former perceptions of geographic peripherality or isolation have now become meaningless. Just as we must redefine these concepts, we are also revisiting the view of growth as being always desirable. This is a new challenge. It is one that will force people in Ennis and other towns to wonder if they should be pleased or dismayed if there is a new factory announced for the town. This is a remarkable turnaround from a position in which essentially any industry was better than no industry. The costs of growth are now becoming increasingly apparent. We are seeing how the unprecedented pace of growth in Ireland is placing ever-increasing stress on the urban infrastructure, making towns and cities increasingly less attractive as places in which to live and work. As a corollary, rural areas may be becoming increasingly attractive to a mobile and globalised population.

One of the ironic consequences of this is that as rural areas increase in their attractiveness, the indigenous rural dwellers are finding it increasingly difficult to live and work there. Related to this, of course, is that people, especially in rural areas, without property are becoming increasingly displaced, in much the same way as the indigenous residents were displaced in inner-city communities through processes of gentrification. Chris Curtin remarks that 'The urban fringe throughout the South of Ireland has tended to worsen the situation of the propertyless and the landless, rural and urban population, as they have been forced to compete in the market, inflated by affluent urban interests and a social structure and culture that is increasingly defined by affluent urban values'.[4] Forces such as these are now beginning to propel us towards exploring a model of development that is holistic and environmentally and socially sustainable, i.e., we are moving from concerns with standard of living to concerns with quality of life.

Erich Fromm[5] distinguishes between a state of 'having' and a state of 'being'. A state of 'having' is a condition whereby self-worth is based on the appurtenances of a consumer age. Attributes that are external to the person assume a core significance in the self-identity of the person. A state of 'being', on the other hand, is one in which the person's identity and self-worth are based on the individual's own innate capacity to achieve a quality of life that is largely independent from one's standard of living. Achieving such a quality of life, in Fromm's terms, is characterised by a level of self-sufficiency, inner peace and the absence of a relentless pursuit of consumer goods. It is based on the distinction between richness and riches and between well-being and acquisitiveness.

Achieving a state of 'being', then, is to aim for personal wholeness or completeness. It assumes an active search in one's own psyche as one progresses through life for the wisdom of detachment as opposed to attachment. At the individual level, according to Fromm, a concern with 'being' rather than having implies the following qualities:

1. Willingness to give up all forms of having, in order to fully *be*.

2. Security, sense of identity, and confidence based on faith in what one is, on one's need for relatedness, interest, love, solidarity with the world around one, instead of on one's desire to have, to possess, to control the world, and thus become the slave of one's possessions.

3. Being fully present where one is.

4. Joy that comes from giving and sharing, not from hoarding and exploiting.

5. Living without worshipping idols and without illusions, because one has reached a state that does not require illusions.

6. Making the full growth of oneself and of one's fellow beings the supreme goal of living.

7. Knowing that no growth is healthy that does not occur in a structure, but knowing, also, the difference between structure as an attribute of life, and 'order' as an attribute of no-life, of the dead.

8. Developing one's imagination, not as an escape from intolerable circumstances but as the anticipation of real possibilities, as a means to do away with intolerable circumstances.

9. Sensing one's oneness with all life, hence giving up the aim of conquering nature, subduing it, exploiting it, raping it, destroying it, and trying, rather, to understand and co-operate with nature.

Is it far-fetched to imagine that the Irish, who have made such a unique and distinctive contribution to the world of art, literature and music throughout history, would evolve an equally distinctive contribution to the understanding of economic development as a process underpinned by a condition of *not having?* In my work as an adult educator I am aware of the increasing number of Irish people who are individually opting for life goals of the form outlined by Fromm. At a wider social level it is more difficult to detect any such trend. This is understandable, perhaps, in a situation in which the prevailing wisdom insists that we have never had it so good. There may be some merit, however, in speculating about what an alternative approach to development as a national project would look like, if based on principles of sustainability and holism.

Principles such as these had little bearing on the approach to development that emerged out of the Industrial Revolution. The factory was the dominant organisational model acquired from the Industrial Revolution.[6] Society began to apply this model to the management of other social problems, especially to the management of problem people. So accompanying the growth of factories, we also witnessed the growth of army barracks, boarding schools, asylums, orphanages, prisons, workhouses, hospitals and schools. They were all driven by the core principle that the most effective way to deal with problems was by concentrating them in a factory-type environment and by applying specialists to the task.

Following on the Cartesian tradition of separating mind and body, and of giving the mind supremacy over the body (I *think* therefore I am rather than I *feel* therefore I am), modern science embarked upon a project of reducing reality to its most minute molecular form. Biotechnology is currently the most advanced application of this approach. This focus on the components rather than on the totality gives rise to specialists. Fundamental to the approach of the specialist is the need to isolate specific problems from the general environment. E. F. Schumacher is reputed to have wondered if a Martian, on visiting the Earth, would be more surprised by the skill of our dentists or the rottenness of our teeth. By confusing dental health with the repair of teeth, we largely ignore the negative role of many food products in overall health or indeed in dental health.

A commitment to holism would have to oppose if not reverse these processes of concentration and specialisation. Holism refers to an approach to reality as an integrated whole, whose properties are more than the sum of its parts and cannot be reduced to those of smaller units. All parts contribute to the whole, interacting together to give a functioning, constantly fluid system, in which:

1. Nothing exists solely by itself;

2. Entities interact with each other in circular patterns rather than in a linear cause-and-effect fashion;

3. There is a reciprocal relationship between all parts of a system.

Perhaps, then, the overriding task of this current generation is to rise above its experience of betrayal and to work towards a collective, conscious decision concerning the nature of its legacy to future generations. Such a concern inevitably raises issues regarding the sustainability of the current development goals. We should not reduce or deplete the capacity of others – whether present or future generations – to meet their goals.

An approach to development from a systemic, holistic perspective would look to the ways in which each element of the system interacts with the others so as to enhance the overall well-being of the system. This would result in a self-generating process, thereby reversing the forces of system depletion. Such a virtuous cycle may be represented diagrammatically as follows:

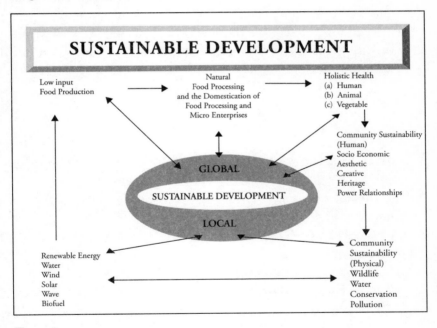

Figure 1

Figure 1 aims to represent an approach to development that is:

Responsible – not wasteful of resources or harmful to the biosphere; relies on resource management rather than resource exploitation.

Overarching – recognises the systematic nature of life and how all actions interact with one another.

Self-generating – momentum is not derived from processes of depletion – environmental, geographic, social or intergenerational.

Enriching – draws attention to the need for each individual to produce as well as to consume.

Perhaps most importantly of all, this diagram draws attention to the fact that economic goals are just one aspect of the development challenge. A singular or even primary focus on economic effectiveness will accentuate problems in other aspects of life and will ultimately, in a curious way, prove unsustainable even on economic grounds.

At the end of the day, we must bear in mind that, just as we are now revisiting the legacy of former generations, so too will future generations revisit ours.

NOTES

1. Michael D. Higgins, *The Betrayal* (Galway: Salmon Publishing, 1990).
2. D. Kiberd, *Inventing Ireland: The Literature of the Modern Nation* (London: Vintage, 1996).
3. A. Giddens, *Beyond Left and Right* (Cambridge: Polity Press, 1994).
4. C. Curtin, T. Haase and H. Toby, *Poverty in Rural Ireland: A Political Economy Perspective,* (Dublin: Combat Poverty Agency, 1996).
5. E. Fromm, *To Have or to Be?* (London: Abacus, 1979).
6. E. Fromm, 'The Nature of Well-Being', in *Awakening the Heart,* edited by John Welwood (Boston: Shambhala Publications, 1983), pp. 59-69.
7. Alvin Toffler, *The Third Wave* (London: Pan Books in Association with Collins, 1981).

5

LOVE AND WORK IN THE MILLENNIUM: A VISION FOR PERSONAL BALANCE AND DEVELOPMENT

MIRIAM MOORE

This is the era of the Celtic Tiger. Material resources for happiness and inner peace have never been greater. Tremendous technological advances and the ensuing flood of production have made luxuries necessities and last year's models antiquated. Yet people do not seem to be any happier because of better plumbing, clothes, refrigerators, cars, cellular phones and all the things they can have and buy. Indeed the contrary may be true.

If we look at the modern workplace, we find that 64 per cent of the people there are dangerously overdosing on self-generated stress hormones, which leaves them emotionally unbalanced, endangers their health and diminishes the quality of their work and their home and family life. According to the World Health Organisation, emotional disorders stemming from work-related stress are among our most serious social problems. Nearly every job is more stressful than it was a decade ago. Stress levels in the workplace, already rated as worryingly high, are predicted to get even higher in the next millennium.

Organisations increasingly recognise that an emotionally balanced, challenged and satisfied workforce is their most important resource, a resource that provides an essential key to keeping the economic scales of business balanced in favour of profit and success. Knowing this, one might ask what is going wrong? Because statistics show that something is getting very out of balance in our workplaces! In terms of human suffering, deteriorating health and diminished quality of life, the costs of this imbalance are inestimable.

At the same time, the financial costs to organisations are enormous. According to a study published last month by the British Institute of Management, work-related illness costs the economy as much as £18 billion per year – equivalent to 2 per cent of GDP. Obviously this is not good for business, and it costs employers somewhere between 5 and 8 per cent of their profits. The study shows that a third of all work-related illnesses is due to anxiety and depression.

In the US it is calculated that work-related depression and anxiety is costing the economy $48 billion a year. And I know from my own practice that there are many anxious and depressed people who stay working but keep silent about their problems for any number of reasons, including fear of stigma or loss of promotion.

These studies do not tell us how many people in the workforce mask their depression and anxiety with other explanations for their absences. Nor do they tell us about the cost to productivity when depressed and anxious employees somehow manage to soldier on, in stressful states of mind. Taking all these factors into account, it is a safe assumption that there are many workplaces where stress is costing employers 10 per cent or more of their profits.

According to Freud, love and work are the two things in life we must do well. When we lose our emotional balance, our inner peace of mind, we tend to do neither well. This loss of emotional/work/life balance is, of course, not good for individuals, for their work, for their families, or for business.

Stress and Distress
First, I would like to make it clear that stress is not harmful. On the contrary, it is a natural and wonderful condition of life. The 'adrenalin rush' that it gives us is exhilarating and can bring out the best in us. It keeps the pendulum of life swinging between the edges of certainty and order, and uncertainty and creative disorder; it is energising, it helps us to rise to the occasion, motivates us to get things done, helps us to think better, and even tones up the body. Stress, by enhancing performance, is not only good for each of us individually; it is also good for business.

Stress can be the spice of life but it can also be the kiss of death. Positive stress can turn negative when it is excessive or prolonged. This negative stress is what happens when we feel that we are losing our emotional balance – when pressures mount and exceed our perceived resources to deal with them. When stress is excessive or prolonged it can be dangerous. Under these conditions the body produces copious amounts of stress hormones called cortisols. These chemicals gunge up our cells and generate a lack of well-being and that 'tired all the time' feeling, which even sleep itself does not restore. Our judgement becomes clouded and we tend to make mistakes and faulty decisions. We observe less, see less, remember less, learn less and generally become less efficient. We are irritable, withdrawn or aggressive, and people find us difficult to work with. When we are over-stressed, instead of working 'smarter', we often work harder and longer and yet produce less.

There is an alarming increase in the incidence of alcoholism, drug abuse and major health breakdown among workers and managers. When occupational stress is ongoing, instead of turning to exercise, meditation or other healthy ways to reduce tension, people will often resort to cigarettes, food binges, alcohol or other drugs to get relief and comfort. And these substances can, in turn, become sources of stress in themselves, further endangering health.

Prolonged or excessive work stress can cause severe mental problems, including PTSD (Post Traumatic Stress Disorder), PDSD (Prolonged Duress Stress Disorder), anxiety, depression, and can even lead to suicide; in Sweden each year, it is believed that over three hundred people commit suicide on account of work-related stress disorders.

One of the dangerous features of stress is its cumulative nature. Disease does not happen suddenly, but is usually a process of development. One doesn't have good health one minute and a massive coronary the next. Continually flooding our bodies with stress hormones can impair our immune system, and render us vulnerable to a host of serious diseases including hypertension and coronaries. As a society we have virtually conquered infectious diseases, but we seem to have replaced them with stress-induced, degenerative diseases. Over half of all premature deaths are related to stress and lifestyle. It is said that most heart attacks tend to occur around 9.00 p.m. on Mondays; this may be telling us something about attitudes to work!

Personal Life

Occupational distress can take its toll on personal lives. Families and partners, for example, are often the hidden victims. Research reveals that only 15 per cent of executives say that their organisations make any attempt to enable them to balance their work and personal life. Over half of them believe that their employers expect it of them to put in long hours.

Living with someone who is enslaved by work and tends to be tired, tense, moody or withdrawn is not easy. Sex becomes a matter of 'thanks for the memories' and this can lead to feelings of rejection and resentment in their partners. Unhappy couples will turn elsewhere for support or tune into the TV and not to each other for a supply of canned laughter, conversation and comfort.

When both parents are victims of work-related stress, the chances of a happy home life are greatly diminished. Home is no longer a place of nurture where one can renew oneself emotionally and replenish energy. Instead it can become an additional cause of stress – perhaps even a place from which to escape.

Several families today suffer from a 'time famine' or a sense of time urgency – too much to do and not enough time to do it. It is estimated that parents spend 40 per cent less time with their children than they did twenty years ago. The time-conscious, 'used up' parent can in many cases present as an out-of-control victim – a poor role model for children, who may wonder about the meaning of it all. And what is the meaning of it all? Why are so many people suffering from such high levels of stress in the workplace?

Major Causes of Workplace Stress

It would be next to impossible to pinpoint all the causes of work-related stress because stress is different for everyone. Nevertheless, I will attempt to outline what I consider to be some of the more conspicuous culprits affecting the majority of people in the workforce.

Organisational Climate

There has been a virtual revolution in the work environment over the past decade. Firms and corporations are often operating under huge pressure to survive. Markets have gone global and the free market brings with it fierce competition. At the same time, shareholders demand more dividends and costs have to be kept to a minimum, so that there is an ever-increasing pressure on the bottom line. Rapid change, downsizing, redundancies and new technologies are the order of the day. It's not surprising that employees are profoundly affected by this highly pressurised climate of dizzying change and insecurity.

Companies are not here to solve the world's problems and if they don't make a profit they are gone and so are the jobs. However, in the urgency to make profits, some companies tend to downgrade the needs of their workforce. In so doing, they are in danger of killing the goose that lays the golden egg. To overlook the needs of the workforce proves to be unprofitable in the long term as the effects of stress and burnout hit home. Every progressive employer knows that making a profit is not mutually exclusive to valuing and developing employees. Indeed, when organisations spend time and money listening to their employees and helping them to develop and respond to change, the productivity rate is higher and so are the profits.

On the other hand, when the needs of employees are not considered and when employees are treated as though they are dispensable commodities to be used up in the quest for power and profit, then the stress levels soar. And when stress levels go up, productivity and profit levels go down. The equation is simple!

Employees thrive and are most productive when the organisational climate is one of *trust and fairness;* where there is a sense of community and satisfying relationships; where communication is authentic; where painful, difficult feelings and issues are not avoided and where differences are bridged with courage and integrity. Employees need to feel that they count, that they are listened to and that they can make decisions affecting their work. They need the opportunity to grow and to develop talents and skills. They also need help to balance their personal and work lives. Rather than just making a living, people need to make a life.

Overload

A major cause of stress is the fact that we are living in times of unprecedented change where the only certainty is that nothing is certain. The momentum of life has speeded up to such an extent that the world of work is becoming an overwhelming place of files, piles, e-mails, cell-phones, telephones, computers, profits and traffic jams; a place where Big Brother is watching to ensure that everyone stays running faster and faster just to stay in the same place. In order to keep running and to keep up, many fill their tense bodies with a variety of poisons – sleeping pills, coffee, antidepressants, tranquillisers, alcohol, nicotine, etc.

Accelerated change, global competition, new technology, downsizing and doing more with less, leave many employees with a great sense of time urgency and the need to work harder and longer. The certainty of 'a job for life' has been replaced by the uncertainty of job change and the need for life-long learning to keep abreast of new skill demands.

Women who work are often forced to turn into workaholics by the sheer volume of work they have to do. Labour-saving devices do not mean that there is less work to do in the home, and women being in the workforce does not mean that men do more work in the home and women do less. There are those who develop an addiction to work to the point that it constantly preoccupies their minds. Workaholics have little time for their children or partners and seldom have friends outside of work unless they are of use to it. They usually justify and rationalise their addiction on the grounds that their work is important or that they are doing it for the good of their family or society, etc. There is usually fear in work addiction. Perhaps fear of standing still and facing gnawing inner tensions and anxieties; fear of loss – loss of approval, loss of promotion, job loss or, perhaps, a fear of acknowledging an unsatisfactory relationship or home life. It has become socially accepted and rewarding to overwork. There can also be peer pressure to give 110 per cent of oneself to work, regardless of the cost to health or personal life. But people, like cars, when driven too hard, will eventually wear out. And again, this is not good for business. In the long term, people who overwork are not as productive and make more unnecessary mistakes than those who work not longer, but smarter.

Organisation Change and Lack of Control
One of the major causes of work-related distress is coping with change. People tend to fear the unknown – 'better to stick with the devil that

you know than commit to the devil that you don't know'. Life is an ongoing dance of kaleidoscopic change. We need the security of certainty and we need the challenge of uncertainty. Too much of either can put us off balance.

When change is imposed or when it happens too quickly, without reassurance, support and due concern for their needs, employees can experience too much uncertainty and feel that they are losing control. They can resent being treated as though they are just objects to be used and manipulated for company expediency and profit. Losing control is probably one of the most horrible feelings in the world. Everyone wants to feel in control of their lives. When we feel that something or someone else is governing what we do and that there is nothing we can do about it, we become life's victims. The result is often fear and powerlessness stemming from the belief that one is unable to be effective or unable to act, or that action itself, even if possible, is futile and doomed to failure.

A phenomenon known as 'learned helplessness' can set in. Like flies trapped in a jar, which do not take flight and escape when the lid is removed, we come to believe that we are powerless and that action is futile. We try to normalise the abnormal. Eventually we do adjust and consider normal the very conditions that oppress us. But at a price! Loss of a sense of control and job insecurity cause great stress and anxiety in the workplace and can eventually lead to serious depression. Research shows that in many companies change is not managed as well as it could be. This results in work climates of fear, distrust and resistance, where relationships deteriorate and stress levels soar. Introducing change in a way that helps employees feel good about it and gets their commitment and co-operation requires great sensitivity and really good communication. It is perhaps one of the most important skills that management needs to acquire in today's world of rapid change.

Fear and Poor Communication

In my experience, the best stress-reliever in the workplace, in addition to satisfying work, is the presence of a sense of community; a climate of trust, open communication, mutual support and laughter. In some companies today, however, fear seems to be a dominant emotion – fear of job loss, fear of lack of promotion, fear of not being able to cope, fear of being seen to be unable to cope, fear of not getting the work done in time, fear of making mistakes, fear of punishment and fear of change. In such an atmosphere, trust and open, honest relationships are lost.

Where fear predominates, employees afraid of being themselves tend to resort to a passive-aggressive form of communication. They bury their real feelings and motives, passively smile and people-please, all the while seething inside with hostility and resentment. However, when feelings are buried, they are buried alive. They demand release and expression and eventually reappear, cloaked in various guises, including masked aggression, bullying, backbiting, intimidation, sarcasm and resistance.

The irony of it all is that modern offices are filled with the most sophisticated electronic equipment, which can spread communication around the world in seconds, and yet, at a human level, employers cannot communicate with employees and colleagues are unable to communicate with each other.

Cultural Values

Overwork, fear, poor communication, enforced change, too much uncertainty, lack of emotional support and powerlessness are just some of the more salient factors contributing to stress and loss of peace of mind in the workplace. I believe, however, that for the most part, they are also expressions of underlying cultural values and beliefs. In Ireland, could we be in danger of mindlessly sliding into the cult of materialism, like the frog when placed in hot water, who will immediately jump out, but will remain and die in water that is very gradually heated to boiling?

Our social culture is increasingly based on material success and acquisition. There is a tendency for people to be evaluated solely for what they have and where they belong on the social scale and how useful they are in the climb up the success ladder. This encourages the development of the acceptable 'marketing personality', when what is important is not who we are, but what we are seen to be. We could become so attuned to being false to ourselves that we might end up not knowing who we really are. And society tends to reward us for material successes regardless of the costs to our well-being.

Could it be that we are losing our way? Are we succumbing to the mistaken belief that freedom and happiness lie outside ourselves and in material success; that the more things we have and the greater our ability to buy and consume, the greater our sense of well-being?

I would like to make it clear that I do not think that money is the root of all evil nor that there is something wrong with material success. Some people have a natural talent for making fortunes and can rank among the world's great humanitarians, giving generously to charity and worthy causes. It is our attitude to these things that can be dangerously faulty. Granted, we need financial security. Money brings choice. Without it life can be degrading and depressing. In the past we have suffered greatly from want and poverty. In many ways we were a traumatised people. We suffered from oppression, famine and emigration, depression, heavy drinking, and at one time we had the highest rate of schizophrenia in the Western world. Unemployment was rampant. Our stresses stemmed not from work but rather from no work. It is wonderful that we have achieved our present state of affluence.

What I am concerned about is the deadening and dulling effect that a mindless, driven pursuit of things and image can ultimately have on us. I am also concerned with the tendency to associate our happiness and our identity with *having more;* more money, more things, more status, more social approval. Grovelling and worshipping at the altar of Mammon, the god of greed, distorts our perceptions and impoverishes our relationship to life.

Given that our basic need for financial security is satisfied, richness is really a state of mind. The American Blackfoot Indians considered the richest man among them to be the one capable of being the most generous. To maintain emotional and mental balance, our aim should not be maximum consumption, but rather sane consumption and never at the expense of giving our hearts away. For truly, what does it profit us if we gain all the rewards that the world has to offer and in the end lose our heart and soul; what does it profit us if we are to lose out on the real riches of life – love, relationships and community, and the time to cultivate them. A life without love and without people who care may be very rich in other things, but in human terms, it is no life at all. And Irish people, despite all their suffering, and maybe even because of it, were always soulful and warm-hearted. They valued community and relationship. Let us protect these priceless treasures! Let us not forget to listen to our hearts. The heart does not find peace in the grasping belief that more is better. Hearts long for truth and simplicity; they hunger for love and meaning and the knowledge that 'our little, nameless, unremembered acts of kindness and of love' have made a difference and that the world is a tiny bit better for our having lived.

Changing Our Minds

According to the psychologist William James, one of the great discoveries of this century is that of the power of the mind; by changing our minds we can change our lives. Our minds, attitudes and beliefs can make us sick or make us happy. Einstein warned us that 'the splitting of the atom has changed everything except our mode of thinking, and thus we are drifting toward unparalleled catastrophe'.

High stress levels in the workplace alert us to the fact that all is not well in the collective mind of the culture. However, the conditions that cause us to lose our balance can also be the very same conditions that present us with opportunities for psychological growth and learning.

We in Ireland don't have to go through life with eyes wide shut. We have a chance now to take stock of the kind of lives we want to live, the kind of people we want to be and the kind of workplaces in which we will work. If we don't like the direction in which we seem to be going, we can change our minds and do something about it now!

Worthy Values

We need to be aware of the values that we live by, for they have a profound effect on our personalities, our choices and our actions. Identifying our real values – not what we think they are or what we would like them to be – can be difficult and it is easy to deceive ourselves. If you want to know what your values are, look at your actual behaviour. You might be convinced that loving relationships and family are more important to you than work. But look and see where you invest your quality time and energy and you will then know what your real priorities are.

You might persuade yourself that you work long hours for financial security for your family. But in fact you might be doing it to buy more expensive items for your house or image. You could be giving your time, your energy, your life in exchange for extra money to buy a few baubles. Thus you could saddle yourself with debts that keep you working even harder and longer. In this way you deprive your partner or your children of what they really need most – your time and your presence. If you are a CEO you might be convinced that your profits are not made at the expense of the well-being of your workforce. Check the stress levels and absentee rates of your workforce to see if you are right.

A New Paradigm

Science is now telling us that nothing in the universe is separate. Everything and everyone is interconnected and interdependent, affecting and being affected by each other. On the global scale we know that we can't destroy the rainforests without repercussions on the rest of life. On the personal level we know that a diseased heart cannot be understood without reference to the whole person – lifestyle, attitudes, etc.

Ilya Prigogene, a Belgian scientist, won the Nobel prize in 1977 for formulating the mathematics to prove the existence of a strange, self-organising energy in nature that expresses itself in movement towards increasingly complex and ever and ever higher orders of life. This mysterious, upward power impels us to become all that we are. In the same way that the acorn has the potential to become an oak tree, we have the potential and the longing to become increasingly more conscious and more compassionately aware of ourselves, of other people, of other creatures and of our environment.

Arising from these discoveries in quantum physics, a new paradigm or value system is emerging. It is based on the concepts of wholeness, relationship, respect for nature, for the feminine, for feelings and intuition, and on the power of that mysterious Intelligence that radiates through and beyond our bodies and out into the universe. Poets, philosophers and mystics have always known about this power, which moves the sun, the moon and the stars, and in which we move and live and have our being.

In the midst of all the frenzy and stress, I see positive change emerging, like a young shoot pushing up between cracks in the cement. I see around me a growing number of people whose attitudes are becoming more open, more tolerant, more authentic; people who are more spiritually and ecologically aware and who are searching for self-knowledge, simplicity, and something more than the material, the measurable, the marketable.

The more employers and employees are in alignment with the values of this emerging paradigm of holism, relationship, inner power and self-worth, the more the workplace will become a place of maximum co-operation, trust, productivity and minimum stress.

Solutions

Workplace stress is set to become an even more significant issue in the coming decade as the new practice of suing employers for work-related stress illness increases. Under the Safety, Health and Welfare at Work Act, 1989, employers are obliged to identify and safeguard against threats to health and safety, and stress is now regarded as a threat to health. Apart from concern about possible litigation, organisations have a great responsibility to ensure that the conditions in which their employees work are favourable to their physical and emotional welfare. It is not only the right thing to do from a humanistic standpoint, it also makes excellent sense economically.

Reducing stress to manageable levels in the workplace means less absenteeism, improved performance, good relationships with colleagues and clients and lower staff turnover. High morale in the workforce is good for business. At the same time, rather than being dependent on organisations to act like parents and take care of their employees, it is essential that employees also begin to be proactive and take responsibility for their own work/life balance and well-being.

One of the most important survival skills for anyone in today's workplace is to learn how to relax physically and unwind and allow the body enough time to repair and recuperate. On the psychological side, it is most important to cultivate 'psychological hardiness'. Stress-resistant people have a specific set of positive attitudes towards life – an openness to change, a sense of control over their lives, a sense of their own worth and a feeling of involvement in whatever they are doing. Over 25 per cent of organisations in the EU are now experimenting with stress-reduction programmes. These usually include education on relaxation methods, diet and exercise, and they can be done effectively with groups.

Cultivating the attitudes of 'psychological hardiness' is more difficult. Managers and staff usually profit from individual help to cope with cumulative or excessive stress. Fortunately, brief therapies are now available that help to release trapped emotional energy and mental blocks and can be very helpful in enabling people to recover their emotional balance. These methods involve using the limbic system or emotional brain with its pathways to the heart. I have found in my work with organisations that some individual counselling sessions, when combined with group work and organisational involvement, can have profound and lasting effects in reducing stress to manageable levels in the workplace.

Individual Power

The workplace, the country, the world, are a collection of individuals. It is by changing consciousness at the individual level that change is effected in the collective consciousness of the group; in the workplace, in the home and even in the entire country. Each of us can ask ourselves what are our priorities. How do we get the balance between work, home and family? Between material needs and relationship? Are our values commensurate with our highest good? Do they nourish our hearts and souls and enhance our development as deeply feeling and compassionate beings? Let us ask ourselves who we are, what is the meaning that we give to life and what really *matters!*

The best gift we can give to life, to work and to relationships is the gift of our own well-being and a sense of our own self-worth. The central responsibility for our inner harmony and balance lies ultimately with each of us individually.

Self-knowledge, self-reverence and self-control, the keys to inner peace and balance, are not achieved without effort and commitment, and sometimes help. Self-knowledge obliges us to communicate with our inner selves; to engage in dialogue with our fears, our conflicts, our anger, our destructive forces – all the feelings that we do not like to acknowledge fully and that, therefore, cause us so much pain. Because we are pain-avoiding creatures, it takes courage to face the truth and embark on the road to inner peace and self-discovery. We can't always control what happens to us. What we can do, however, is learn how to control our own responses, thoughts and feelings and cultivate an inner calm and balance.

Life is an adventure, full of wonder, beauty and joy. But it is also difficult. To quote Woody Allen, 'Life is full of unhappiness, miserableness, loneliness and pain . . . and it's all over much too quickly!' However, if each of us individually learned how to face life's pains and challenges from a centre of our inner power and calm, then each of us could make a difference in our place of work and in our relationships!

Like many people in the workplace, you might feel powerless and believe that you as one lone individual can't make any difference. But you can!

A VIEW FROM THE CHAIR

JOHN CUSHNAHAN

The session that I had the honour of chairing featured two very different presentations, the first from sociologist Dr Tom Collins and the second from clinical psychologist Dr Miriam Moore. Both lectures, which were influenced by the personalities and professional disciplines of their respective authors, were stimulating and thought-provoking.

In his paper entitled 'Ireland: The Challenges of Success', Tom Collins explored three ideas and the interrelationship between them, namely democracy, sustainability and holism. He identified these issues as the locale for some of the fundamental challenges confronting Ireland today. With regard to democracy, he made the case for a new type of governance based on a more rigorous approach to the legitimisation of power on the part of the citizenry and a recognition that democracy and citizenship require a proactive engagement of the populace in communal problem-solving.

With regard to sustainability, Tom argued that the development challenge, now that we appear to have solved the 'standard of living' conundrum, is about 'quality of life' issues. The case for an alternative vision for the development of the West, or indeed for rural development, was particularly highlighted. As concern with 'quality of life' issues incorporates concern with holism, Tom concluded with an analysis of this concept, particularly in its capacity to inform the development of person-centred professions.

In her paper entitled 'Love and Work in the Millennium: A Vision for Personal Balance and Development', Miriam Moore stated that we live in times of unprecedented change, when the only certainty is that nothing is certain. She took up a number of issues during her address. She pointed out that a growing number of people – approximately two-thirds of the workforce – are dangerously overdosing on self-generated stress hormones. She examined the reasons for work-related imbalance. She outlined what can happen when the competing demands of work and personal life are not properly managed. She emphasised that, while we can't always control what happens to us, we can learn how to gain control over our own emotional responses.

Miriam contended that the conditions that cause us to lose our balance can be the very same conditions that present us with opportunities for sociological growth. Accordingly, learning this can motivate us to look for our power and equilibrium deep within the centre of our being, and she examined this in some detail. Not surprisingly, we were told that the road to emotional mastery and inner balance is not always easy – it can often be blocked by deeply conditioned limiting beliefs, conflicts and unresolved hurts that reason and willpower alone fail to budge.

Miriam discussed new approaches to removing these blocks and how they can help us all to achieve a healthier balance between life and work. When applied to the workplace, the maintenance of this balance will create energised workplaces where productivity operates at its maximum level, stress is of a positive nature and absenteeism is non-existent.

Before our particular session commenced I had been somewhat apprehensive, due to the fact that the previous day's proceedings, particularly the contribution from Dr Stephen Covey, had created such a 'buzz'. I was therefore concerned that our proceedings could result in something of an anti-climax. However, my fears were misplaced due to the excellent contributions from Tom and Miriam. They responded to the challenge magnificently and both of their presentations were warmly received by the audience.

The two papers were markedly different, in both approach and topic itself. It was therefore difficult to compare and analyse them for common themes. In his remarks, Tom explored a number of issues related to structural problems in society and the relationship between them. On the other hand, Miriam's theme focused more on personal development, work-related success and how organisations can help individuals to achieve a healthier work/life balance.

The diversity and wide-ranging nature of the two papers prompted an equally diverse set of questions from the floor. Issues raised included globalisation, participative democracy, asylum seekers, the perceived policy of Clare County Council to restrict planning permission to those born in the 'banner county' and the current spate of scandals in political, business and Church life.

In conclusion, I would like to say how impressed I was with the commitment and concentration of the audience. Despite the fact that we were well into the second day of the conference, during which some very serious topics had been discussed, their interest and enthusiasm remained undiminished. They responded to the request for reflection in a disciplined and dignified manner. They participated in the question-and-answer session with great eagerness.

The message is quite simple – the success of this conference depended as much on the participation of the audience as it did on the quality of the contributions of the main speakers.

6

THE GROWTH ILLUSION

Richard Douthwaite

When you consider that in the past twelve years total incomes in Ireland have grown by almost as much as they had previously grown in the entire six-thousand-year span of this country's history, it's apparent that something extraordinary is going on. But however extraordinary it may be, is it worth it? Are we really twice as well off as we were in 1987? What are ordinary people getting out of the rapid changes taking place, apart from increased stress, further damage to the natural environment and worse traffic congestion? Oh, and a property boom that has had the effect of ensuring that many couples can't afford to buy a house even if both partners go out to work.

To put this another way, what do we expect economic growth to do for us? Not so long ago, we wouldn't have had any doubt about the answer. It was to lift people out of poverty and enable them to have both a higher standard of living and a better quality of life. Political parties dressed these expectations up in different ways: those on the left would talk about growth leading to higher wages, improved social welfare, better hospitals, a lower pupil-teacher ratio and so on, while those on the right would stress greater profits and a wider range of choice.

Some parties still talk in these terms: 'Our shared ambition is to make Ireland one of the most dynamic countries in the world with a quality of life which is second to none; the key to further growth and stability is continued partnership and mutual self-restraint; for every year that high growth continues, we can put more people to work, cut taxes and provide money for improved infrastructure and social services', the Taoiseach, Mr Ahern, said in his address to the Fianna Fáil Ardfheis in November 1998. Quite obviously, he does not see any conflict between a high level of dynamism and a high quality of life, or between further growth and stability.

But, for many people, the old confidence and optimism about the results of the growth process have gone, and rightly so. After all, would anybody looking forward to a doubling of Irish national income in 1987 ever have thought that, once it was achieved, an Irish health board would still be closing hospital wards and sacking nurses for lack of funds, as happened this time last year? This year, of course, hospitals haven't had to sack nurses – they just haven't been able to pay enough to hire them.

Certainly, better-informed politicians no longer speak glowingly of the benefits of growth. I recently did a computerised search of every speech Tony Blair has made since he became British Prime Minister to see if he had ever linked growth with improvements in the lives of ordinary people. He has not. Today, the only benefits that he, and we, should expect from economic growth are increased business profits and – if the rate of growth is fast enough – extra jobs. We should also expect to pay for these benefits through lower wages and greater job insecurity because of the way the globalised economic system, which we joined to generate growth in the first place, works. What's more, achieving growth through the global system exposes both us personally and Ireland as a whole to much higher levels of financial and environmental risk.

So, why, since the benefits of growth have these hefty price-tags attached, is it still considered so important to achieve it? One reason is that firms are constantly trying to lower their costs by introducing labour-saving technologies. The new methods they use cost jobs, which means that every year, unless the total amount of activity in the economy increases by around 3 per cent, unemployment will rise. In the employment area, therefore, the economy has to expand pretty quickly just to stand still.

The second reason this country needs growth is that between 15 and 20 per cent of the Irish population is employed at any time on investment projects designed to expand the economy in the coming years. If growth fails one year, firms that have invested but haven't been able to increase their sales in the flat market will find themselves with surplus capacity. They will therefore axe any further investment plans they might have, causing the people who would have built their new factories and shopping centres to be put out of work. And, since these newly unemployed people will obviously have less to spend, further jobs will be lost in other sectors of the economy. This will cause consumer spending to fall even more and cause more job losses. In short, a downward spiral could develop, leading to a serious depression.

The possibility of this happening terrifies every government in the world to such an extent that they are prepared to do almost anything to ensure that growth carries on. In Ireland's case, successive governments have adopted a policy of generating growth through foreign direct investment. As a result, they have had to maintain the country's attractiveness to transnational corporations by demanding sacrifices from the majority of the population whenever required. International competitiveness has had to be preserved at almost any cost.

This simple piece of analysis explains a lot of what has happened in Ireland recently. Look at the papers. Scarcely a day goes by without a politician or business person announcing that, unless the road network is improved, or social welfare benefits reduced in real terms so that taxes can be cut, or the use of genetically modified organisms permitted, or the school curriculum made more relevant to the workplace, or the rate of increase in wages controlled by means of another national pay agreement, the economy will become uncompetitive in world markets. In other words, we are being told that unless we give up or change something important to us, we, or to those close to us, might find ourselves impoverished and/or out work.

Essentially, we are being threatened, and historians looking for a handy way of spotting the point at which Irish economic growth ceased to be of benefit to the broad mass of the population have only to look for the point at which credible promises of a rosier future were out-numbered by phrases that started with 'unless' and didn't pretend that a brighter tomorrow would come about even if we went along with whatever was being proposed. Remember the scare stories we were told to ensure we voted in favour of the Maastricht Treaty and the Single European Act?

As with other forms of blackmail, these threats will never end if we

give in to them. This is because other countries are continually being
asked to make environmental, financial and social sacrifices to
maintain their competitiveness too. If we agree to allow a motorway to
be built, or social welfare provisions to be eroded in real terms,
pressure will be put on other countries to provide equivalent financial
savings for firms operating there. If they do, the pressure for further
subsidies and environmental sacrifices will switch back to us.

Round and round the cycle of immiseration will go, screwing the
majority down and leaving only a very wealthy minority better off.
The process has gone depressingly far already. The UNDP's 1999
Human Development Report showed that in the past four years, the
world's two hundred richest people have doubled their wealth to more
than $1,000 billion, while the number of people living on less than a
dollar a day has remained unchanged at 1.3 billion. 'Global
inequalities in income and living standards have reached grotesque
proportions', the report said. Thirty years ago, the gap between the
richest fifth of the world's people and the poorest was 30:1. By 1990,
it was 60:1 and today it is 74:1.

Devaluations apart, the main way Irish governments have
improved the country's competitiveness has been to use successive
national agreements to keep wages down. For example, the present
agreement, Partnership 2000, provided for general pay increases of
only 2.5 per cent in its first year, 2.25 per cent in its second year and
a total of 2.5 per cent given in two stages six months apart in its final
year, which ends on 1 April 2000. As these increases are scarcely more
than the rate of inflation, workers' incomes have inevitably fallen
further behind those of the better off, particularly as the total income
of all the groups that comprise the Irish economy can be expected to
go up by 8 per cent or more annually in the years to which Partnership
2000 applies. In short, because of the way that successive Irish
governments have chosen to bring it about, growth in Ireland is no
longer about increasing the earnings of the whole population. The
system actively prevents the less-well-off from getting more than a few
crumbs.

It's true that under Partnership 2000, workers could negotiate local
agreements with their employers to give them a maximum of another
2 per cent a year. However, this doesn't change the picture, as these

extra payments are rarely conceded for nothing. 'The most common trade-offs for higher pay [are] acquiescence to more part-time work, more temporary work, more fixed-term contracts, more sub-contracting and new technologies', Denis O'Hearn, a sociologist at Queen's University, Belfast, wrote in his 1998 book, *Inside the Celtic Tiger*.[1]

It's also true that tax rates have been cut as part of national wage agreements to boost workers' take-home pay. Between 1987 and 1997, these cuts added 9 per cent to gross industrial earnings in real terms, a significant subsidy to employers if you consider that, after inflation, the increase they gave their workers amounted to only 15 per cent. In sum, workers' earnings rose by 24 per cent in real terms in a period in which the total incomes of the nation rose by three times that amount. But the national wage agreements were great from the employers' point of view. By keeping the cost of employing people down between 1990 and 1999, they enabled firms to cut the labour component of the cost of each item produced by 40 per cent.[2]

These cuts in tax rates reduced the total tax-take in Ireland to far below the average EU level. Ireland collected 41 per cent of GDP in taxes in 1986, but only 34 per cent in 1996. Amongst our partners, however, the take rose from 45 per cent to 46 per cent over the same period. If we can't pay for a proper health service or social welfare system, this is why. But even this reduction is not enough for some, including the US economist Jeffrey Sachs, best-known for promoting an extreme form of capitalism in the former Soviet bloc. A NESC report, *Sustaining Competitive Advantage*, published in March 1998, records that Sachs 'notes that Ireland has a much higher level of taxation and public expenditure than its Asian competitors'. As I said, the screwing-down will go on and on.

Not only have Irish employees not had their pay increased very much since 1986, they haven't gained a shorter working week or longer paid holidays either. Indeed, the recent resurgence in France apart, the international movement towards working fewer hours each year seems to have been stopped in the early eighties by the pressures of globalisation. The 1,810 hours that the average Irish employee works in a year is longer than anywhere else in the EU except Greece and Portugal, and shows little sign of coming down.

The most recent distribution of income figures for Ireland is for 1994, so it's impossible to say definitively where the extra income generated by more recent growth has gone. However, it's safe to say that a major chunk – around 14 per cent – went to transnational companies based here, and as they send it back home, it never entered the Irish economy at all. Indeed, it was actually harmful to us because it is included in the figure used by the EU in determining this country's eligibility for structural funds and other grants. Ireland's national income has risen to the average for the rest of the EU only if the transnationals' profits are included.

As profits in Irish-owned businesses have gone up sharply, a lot of the rest of the growth must have gone to the richest 30 per cent of the population who, in 1994, already enjoyed 55 per cent of Irish incomes, while the poorest 30 per cent rubbed along on only 10.4 per cent between them. This supposition is partially confirmed by figures from the Central Bank, which show that between 1988 and 1998, profits, rents and dividends went up by 3.6 times in money terms, whereas wages, salaries and pensions went up by only 2.3 times. Even so, we don't know exactly how much of this country's income the richest 20 per cent are getting now, but in the United States, between 1979 and 1995, the incomes of the wealthiest 20 per cent rose by 26 per cent, the middle 20 per cent by 1 per cent and the bottom 20 per cent actually saw their incomes decrease by 9 per cent.

Even at the 1994 level, Ireland had the second-least equal distribution of earnings among the member-nations of the OECD – the US was the worst. Ireland was also second-worst for the number of full-time wage-earners living in relative poverty because they earned less than two-thirds of the median wage. 'In Ireland, 21 per cent of employees were low-paid in 1987 and by 1994 this had risen to 24 per cent', a 1997 report by the Economic and Social Research Institute says.[3] Again, the US beat this figure, with 25 per cent. Ireland didn't have to become less equal during those years; it was the development path our politicians chose. Between 1987 and 1994, the gap in earnings narrowed in Germany, Belgium, Finland, Japan and Canada. It is hardly surprising that many Irish workers now feel that they were sold out by their union negotiators in the national wage agreements.

What we can definitely say about Ireland is that the rich have got richer and that the poor have got poorer in relation to the rich. This is serious even if the poor aren't living in absolute poverty, because being poor in relation to other members of one's society damages one psychologically. It consequently affects one's physical health and shortens one's life expectancy.

Richard Wilkinson of the Trafford Centre for Medical Research at the University of Sussex has spent over twenty years studying how changes in people's relative incomes affect their health (see figure 1). He has found that in countries where incomes have become more equal, the incidence of disease has fallen and life expectancy has gone up. These improvements were not the result of economic growth, better health care, or the movement of individuals out of absolute poverty, he says. 'There are too few people in absolute poverty in each of the developed countries for their death rates to be the decisive influence [on the statistics].'

He adds that since the early 1970s, Japan has gone from the middle of the field in terms of life expectancy and income distribution to the top in both. 'Japan now has the highest recorded life expectancy and

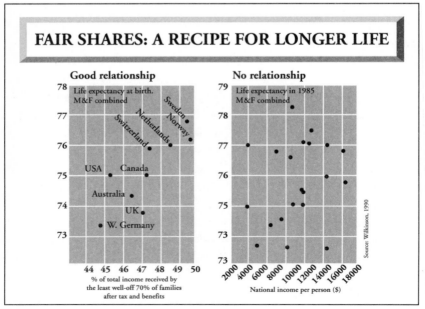

Figure 1

the most egalitarian income distribution in the world', he says. 'On the other side of the coin, while Britain's income distribution worsened dramatically during the eighties to produce the largest inequalities for over a century, its relative position in terms of life expectancy has also worsened. Each year since 1985, mortality rates among both men and women between the ages of sixteen and forty-five have actually risen – a trend which is not attributable to AIDS.'

In other words, Britons – and, almost certainly, Irish people too – are dying prematurely not because they don't have enough to live on but because the distribution of resources has become less fair. Why is someone's relative income level important enough to cause this? 'Relative poverty is a demeaning and devaluing experience', Wilkinson says, arguing that the way people feel about themselves has a major effect on their health.

He believes that once an adequate level of national output has been reached, the best way to make people feel better is not to produce more and more goods for them to consume, but to share incomes – and therefore goods – more equally. '[This] might be expected to improve the quality of life for everyone by simultaneously improving the social fabric and slowing the pace of environmental damage', he says.

In the US it has been found[4] that states with greater inequality of income also have a greater proportion of babies born with low birth weight; higher rates of homicide; higher rates of violent crime; a greater proportion of the population unable to work because of disabilities; a higher proportion of the population using tobacco; and a higher proportion of the population being sedentary (inactive). These states also had higher costs per person for medical care, and higher costs per person for police services.

Unfortunately, no one in Ireland seems to be investigating the effects of changes in the income distribution on people's health to see if anything similar is happening here. One of the first effects of an increase in inequality would be a rise in the number of babies weighing less than 5.5 lb at birth. Research by Professor David Barker, an epidemiologist at Southampton University, has shown that underweight babies are much more likely to develop heart disease, high blood pressure, diabetes and kidney and liver problems in later life. This may be because their bodies diverted the poor supply of nutrients their mothers provided in the womb away from their vital organs to ensure that their brains, at least, developed fairly well. Some workers think, however, that their brains could be permanently locked in 'fight or flight' mode. If true, this could partially explain the high incidence of crime and behavioural problems among deprived groups.

From the national point of view, the birth of an underweight baby is a double tragedy. It is bad for the community, who will have to shoulder the expense of providing medical – and possibly custodial – care for the new individual for a lot of his or her life. It is worse, however, much worse, for the baby concerned, as it will have to put up with chronic illnesses and never develop its full potential. This being the case, is the Irish government constantly monitoring the incidence of low birth weight? Not at all. The most recent published figures[5] are for 1993. I'm told that all the hospitals' returns for the years since then are piled in a Department of Health office waiting to be processed.

There is reason to be worried about what the results might show. In 1998, the Southern Health Board stated[6] that the unsatisfactory infant mortality figures for Cork city were caused by low birth weight, congenital abnormalities and infant death syndrome. It associated these with the high levels of social deprivation in the city. Currently, Britain has the highest proportion of underweight babies in the EU, 7.2 per cent, worse than Albania (6.9 per cent) and Latvia (5.2 per cent). Out of more than thirty-five European countries surveyed by the World Health Organisation, the only nations with higher proportions of underweight babies were Bulgaria (9.1 per cent), Romania, Hungary (both 9 per cent), and Turkey (7.5 per cent). It would be a terrible condemnation of the path this country has taken recently if, when they are eventually calculated, the Irish figures are found to be worse.

Many Irish social indicators have certainly worsened since the 1970s, as the Fordham Index of Social Health for Ireland shows. This was compiled by Catherine Kavanagh of University College, Cork, who based her work on the original index that has been compiled each year since 1985 by Marc Miringoff and colleagues at the Fordham University Graduate Center, Tarrytown, New York. Miringoff's index monitors sixteen indicators in an effort to assess people's well-being at each stage of their lives. For children, it reports infant mortality, child abuse and poverty; for young people, it covers teenage suicides, drug use, and the high-school drop-out rate; for adults, it follows unemployment, average weekly earnings, and the proportion of those under sixty-five covered by health insurance. For the elderly, it reports poverty and the level of healthcare costs they are required to pay. And for all groups, it covers homicides, alcohol-related road deaths, food-stamp coverage, access to affordable housing and the gap between rich and poor.

Each statistic for each year is not compared with an impossible target, such as zero homicides, but with the best figure the US has achieved for that particular category since 1970. Thus if the homicide figure for 1996 was equal to the best previous year, it would score 100. Similar calculations are made for each statistic and then an average calculated to give the overall index for the year. The recent returns have been disquieting. From 1970 (the first year for which the calculation was done) to around 1977, the index was steady at over 70 per cent. There was then a rapid decline to a new stable level of around 40 per cent, which persisted between 1985 and 1994, the most recent year for which figures have been published. It is, of course, very easy to quibble about these findings. For example, why should all the factors be given an equal weighting? Who says that there should only be sixteen factors anyway? And why do they have to be these particular ones? But despite these valid questions, because the index registers a massive overall decline across so many areas, it can scarcely be denied that the well-being of many Americans must have deteriorated.

Anxious to see if anything similar has happened in Ireland, Dr Kavanagh adapted Miringoff's index for local conditions by dropping indicators that were specific to US conditions and substituting more appropriate ones. For example, she dropped health insurance coverage for adults, the healthcare costs of the elderly, and food-stamp coverage and replaced these with teenage pregnancies, net migration and medical card coverage. In addition, she was unable to include changes in the equality of income distribution in her study because no annual data was available. This left her with fifteen factors rather than the original sixteen. She changed three factors slightly. Alcohol-related road deaths became all traffic accidents, average weekly wages became real hourly earnings, and affordable housing became 'social housing needs' – the number of people either in social housing or eligible for it.

So what did her index show when it was published by the Conference of Religious in Ireland in 1996? Basically, that the well-being of Irish people declined between 1977 and 1983 but then rose slowly so that by 1994 it was back at the 1977 level. Which, of course, means that if changes in income distribution brought about by the growth process had been included, the overall well-being of Irish society would have been shown to have declined.

If those in average jobs haven't done well out of growth, did the unemployed fare better? After all, unemployment is also a demeaning and devaluing experience and it might be fair enough to restrict wage increases if that enabled more people to find work. So how effective has the 'keep wages down to entice the multinationals to locate here' strategy been as a way of generating employment?

The short answer is: Modestly effective. Certainly the approach can claim to have enabled the Republic to come close to maintaining employment levels in its manufacturing sector between 1980 and 1993. Both Britain and Northern Ireland, where industry was not pampered to anything like the same extent, experienced falls of around one-third during the same period. Between 1994 and 1997, however, the total number of people employed in foreign-owned manufacturing plants here rose by roughly 40,000 or 12 per cent. A remarkable figure, yes, but one that looks less remarkable when you realise that 170,000 jobs were created in Irish manufacturing companies, the building trade and other parts of the service sector during the same period.

So if you want to know who or what led to the fall in unemployment recently, the answer is that it wasn't the multinationals or our international competitiveness. It was us. My local paper, *The Mayo News*, shows how. Ten years ago, it might have carried three advertisements from local taxi proprietors: this week it carries eighteen. A local jeweller has taken a three-page spread, as has a new furniture store. And smaller announcements from firms in the home-improvement business appear on nearly every page. Last November, no less than twenty-one hotels and restaurants advertised their Christmas menus, double the number of a decade ago. This year, given that two new hotels have opened, there'll be even more.

Transnationals like Intel and Pfizer aren't providing the wages that keep these service-sector firms in business. Sure, they're contributing, but as we've seen, their employees' incomes have hardly soared. Instead, the bill for our unprecedented spending spree is being met, directly or indirectly, in the same way the boom was paid for in Thailand – by people getting themselves or their companies heavily into debt. Between July 1998 and July this year, the amount Irish residents owed to financial institutions soared by 32.2 per cent or almost £21 billion.[7] This means that in a twelve-month period we borrowed a sum not far short of twice the total amount the government spent in 1996, and appreciably more than the £8 billion bribe the EU paid us to vote for Maastricht.

A lot of this money reached the pockets of non-borrowers via the property boom; the amount outstanding on residential mortgages went up by £3 billion during the year ended April 1999.[8] Many of the new mortgages were taken out by well-off people buying, with the help of tax concessions, holiday homes or apartments to let. As a result, people on the average industrial wage found themselves priced completely out of the market. The latest DKM Housing Affordability Index[9] shows that a Dublin couple on twice average earnings who borrow 90 per cent of the price of their first home now have to pay 33 per cent of their after-tax income to cover their mortgage, compared with about 16 per cent of their income as recently as 1994. Young would-be housebuyers have therefore been hit badly by one of the causes and consequences of recent growth. 'We're competing against our children', a prospective second-home owner told me recently, but he bought the house he was inspecting nonetheless.

A few years ago, the government would have been able to moderate this unsustainable borrowing splurge, but it no longer has that power. It gave it up in order to participate in the Euro in the belief that this would encourage further growth. In other words, the need for growth now gets in the way of the needs of ordinary people. Growth has become our master rather than our servant.

Sometime, perhaps quite soon, the borrowing surge will peak. When this happens, less new money will get into circulation, making it harder for firms to make profits and for everyone to pay their bills. This will cause business confidence to slump and borrowing to fall further, thus setting in motion exactly the type of damaging positive feedback that Irish governments hoped that their growth-through-competitiveness strategy would avoid. Once borrowing and investment fall, all the jobs created in the past few years could be lost – and then some more. In short, the Celtic Tiger and the strategy of generating growth by pandering to the multinationals are totally unsustainable.

Even if the boom ends with a soft landing, the method Ireland is using to generate growth cannot be continued for much longer. The distribution of income here is already the second-least equal in the developed world (the US is worst) and cannot be skewed much further without social strife. The NESC report I referred to earlier mentions 'the difficult challenge of addressing the problem of social cohesion while simultaneously achieving cost competitiveness'. If we hold some groups down for too long, society will tear itself apart.

Our recent growth has been unsustainable in other ways, too. The *Environment in Focus* report issued by the Environmental Protection Agency in June this year stated that habitat loss and changes in agricultural methods had pushed eight bird species to the brink of extinction. Indeed, it suspects that the corn bunting, which was last seen in the Mayo/Galway area in the early nineties, may have already gone. Three types of freshwater fish and one amphibian, the natterjack toad, are also under threat. Only 67 per cent of Irish rivers are now classified as unpolluted, 10 per cent fewer than a decade ago.

But the most serious damage that Irish growth is currently doing to the environment is probably on a global level rather than on a national one because of our total failure to keep our greenhouse gas emissions in check. There is a broad scientific consensus that, because humanity is burning large quantities of fossil fuels and thus releasing more carbon dioxide and other greenhouse gases than can be taken up by the Earth's natural absorption mechanisms, the global climate is likely to change for the worse, if it is not already doing so. The United Nations believes that a 60 to 80 per cent cut in world greenhouse gas emissions is necessary to stabilise the situation and has called a series of international conferences to work out how such a cut can be brought about. At one of these conferences at Kyoto in 1997, the EU signed a protocol on behalf of all of its fifteen member states, which committed them collectively to make an 8 per cent cut in the EU's overall CO_2 emissions from the 1990 level by 2010.

In June 1998, when the responsibility for making this cut happen was divided up, the Irish government agreed to prevent its emissions from rising more than 13 per cent above its 1990 level, leaving its partners with all the problems of actually cutting their energy use back. Shortly afterwards, it gave the go-ahead for the construction of two cement works that, by one estimate,[10] took up all the permitted increase in emissions by themselves. This, plus the increased energy demand generated by the country's unprecedented economic growth, led Pablo Benevides, the director-general of energy at the European Commission, to predict only eleven months later that Irish emissions were likely to overshoot the rise agreed with its partners by 27 to 47 per cent of the 1990 baseline.[11] Other member governments were likely to overshoot too but by smaller amounts, largely because emissions from the EU transport sector were on course to be 39 per cent above the 1990 level. A rapid growth in aircraft emissions was part of this problem.

The damage likely to be done by these additional Irish emissions is likely to be far greater than the benefits from burning the fossil fuels that generated them. This is because the benefits from the fuel use are a one-off, while the damage that the gases do continues for as long as they stay in the atmosphere, which could be thousands of years. The damage that excess emissions are doing globally is already apparent. The warmest year by far for at least 600 years, according to tree rings and ice-core evidence, was 1998. It was nearly half a degree Celsius warmer than the second-warmest year, 1997. 'The extreme warmth of 1998 was accompanied by the signs of climate chaos', Peter Montague wrote in *Rachel's Environmental & Health Weekly*.[12] He went on:

> Record-setting forest fires in Florida, Indonesia, Brazil, Russia, and southern Europe; bush fires in northern Australia; floods and accompanying mudslides in California and coastal Peru and Ecuador (where 50,000 were left homeless); major flooding in east Africa; Hurricane Mitch, which killed more than 20,000 people in Honduras, Nicaragua, and El Salvador and devastated the economies of central America; drought in New Guinea;

intense drought and famine in southern Sudan; drought in central America that left the Panama Canal too shallow for many ships to pass through; failed coffee crops in Indonesia and in Ethiopia; failed sugar and rice crops in Thailand; failed cocoa and rubber crops in Malaysia; cotton crop failure in Uganda; and warm ocean currents that reduced the Peruvian fish catch by 45 per cent.

Paul Epstein of Harvard Medical School estimated[13] that in the first eleven months of 1998, weather-related losses totalled $89 billion, and that 32,000 people died and 300 million were displaced from their homes. This was more than the total losses experienced in the 1980s, he said.

Fossil energy use is very closely linked with economic growth. Indeed, Malcolm Slesser of the Resource Use Institute of Dunblane, Scotland, estimates that 55 per cent of the energy that people in industrialised countries consume is required by the growth process itself. This is because, although in cash terms these countries use only about 18 per cent of everything they make to generate growth, in energy terms the proportion is much higher because the production of steel, aluminium and cement is very energy-intensive. As a result, if we can devise an economic system that does not need continual investment to keep itself from collapse, we can cut our energy consumption very considerably. After all, as figure 2 shows, the amount of energy actually required to feed, clothe and house a human is not very high. Our problem is that we have created a system that makes it so by transporting so much of what we consume from place to place.

Figure 2 shows that transport consumed almost as much energy as the other industrial sectors put together. Indeed, a Spanish study has shown that when all the energy used, directly and indirectly, by transport is taken into consideration – the power required to make the cars, trucks, trains, ships and aircraft, and to build roads, carparks, track, docks and airports for them, and then to provide the cardboard cartons, shipping containers and other packaging materials that moving goods around requires – the sector consumes over half of all fossil energy used in Spain. Slesser's estimate and the Spanish study

Energy use by sector in Britain, 1984

	Value of output (£million)	Energy use (million therms)	Therms/ £100 output
Transport	23,609	14,999	63.53
Iron and steel	7,276	2,935	40.34
Chemicals, syn. fibres	19,573	3,659	18.69
Glass, concrete, etc.	7,743	1,440	18.60
Wood, water, rubber	10,335	1,506	14.57
Non-ferrous metals	3,741	502	13.42
Paper, print, publishing	15,326	820	5.35
Food, drink, tobacco	33,948	1,584	4.67
Cars, ships, aerospace	18,265	712	3.90
Textiles, clothing	11.488	441	3.84
Agriculture	14,375	550	3.83
Mechanical engineering	28,060	1,042	3.71
Electrical engineering	20,958	446	2.13
Construction	43,850	409	0.93

Figure 2
Source: Institute of Fiscal Studies, Commentary No. 19 (January 1990).

obviously count some of the same activities, so their percentages cannot be added together. Nevertheless, they do show that an economy without growth and with very much less transportation would require significantly less energy.

Slesser's estimate explains why economic growth and increased energy use have been inseparable since the start of the industrial revolution, namely, that energy has been required to create the capital assets required to bring growth about. But there is also a second link. All human activity involves the use of energy, and most economic growth has come about either from the monetarisation of activities that were previously done for nothing or through the progressive substitution of increasing amounts of fossil energy for that from human, animal and other renewable sources. For example, a tractor uses fossil fuel rather than the biomass energy required by a horse. So in order to generate growth, fossil energy is required both to build the new equipment and then to keep it running. It is spent both as capital and income. As a result, there is a close relationship between the level of energy used in a country and the level of activity measured by its GNP.

The reason we are emotionally attached to growth and why we find it so hard to say it should stop is that everybody feels that if they had a little bit more of something they would be better off. What we fail to realise is that what is possible for one person is probably not possible for all and if everybody gets a little bit more it may alter or destroy not only the expected benefits but also those that people enjoyed before the change. Growth is a dynamic process, and after it has happened, the world is a different place. It is easy, and valid, for one person to say that, as things stand, if he had a car he would be better off because it would be quicker and more pleasant than walking to the bus through the wind and rain. But the process of giving a car to that person and to everyone else who wants one changes the situation so drastically that it is not possible to say whether, after the process has been completed, the community as a whole will be better off and the new car owners will get the benefits they thought they would. The increase in traffic might lengthen journey times to such an extent that the new car owners take longer to get to work than they did before. Other people's journey times will almost certainly go up as a result of congestion and the total time the community spends travelling to work could increase. Bus frequencies may be cut and fares raised for lack of demand. Thus, even though GNP will increase because of the extra spending on transport, it is possible, even probable, that the country as a whole will be worse off in welfare terms and that many people will be running their cars largely out of necessity because of the way things have developed and not because they like doing so.

Similarly, if the process of growth alters the distribution of income in a country – and particularly if it makes it less equitable as it has done in Ireland – we can't conclude that, just because overall consumption is higher, overall well-being has gone up too. Even if everybody's income goes up equally, living standards need not improve because the increased spending power could be exhausted bidding up the prices of consumer goods whose supply cannot be increased sufficiently to match the demand. These could be cottages in the country, membership of smart clubs, access to fashionable schools or fishing rights in Connemara. The old analogy that if everybody sitting in a theatre stands up to get a better view, nobody gets any advantage, applies exactly to this case. And if there are some people who cannot stand up because their income has not increased to the same extent as everybody else's – pensioners and the unemployed, perhaps – their view will become considerably worse. Even though they may have a little more money than before, they will not be able to afford to maintain their former position.

I know Harry Bohan wanted this paper to be more than an attack on growth and to suggest some alternative approaches, so here goes. The first thing we need to do to achieve a better balance between our economic and social objectives, and between our economic system and the planet's environment, is to accept that the rate of increase in national income is a very poor guide to anything at all except the potential for making a profit. Our well-being depends on very much more than the amount of money we earn, which is one of the reasons that we don't feel much better-off despite all the growth that has taken place. It could be that what we've gained on the swings as a result of higher incomes, we've lost on the roundabouts, because, for example, community and family life have declined. If we really want to know whether the sum total of all the aspects of life that contribute to our well-being is rising, we cannot rely on the GNP growth figure to tell us. We need to measure each one directly, which is what I hope the new research centre will do.

Although most mainstream economists now accept that the rate of growth has little or nothing to do with human welfare, they have only come to think that way within the past four or five years. For example, two economists from the ESRI, Professor Brian Nolan and Tony Fahey, issued a statement pointing out the weakness of the link as recently as March 1996. A few years before that, such a declaration would have been quite unthinkable. Indeed, in 1972, two leading economists, James Tobin, who went on to win a Nobel Prize, and William Nordhaus compiled an index of economic welfare in an attempt to show that it was so closely correlated with GNP that it was a waste of time assembling it on an annual basis. They came away convinced that it was.

Since then, however, something seems to have changed in the way the economic system operates. In the late 1980s, Clifford Cobb built on Nordhaus and Tobin's work to produce a graph that plotted an 'Index of Sustainable Economic Welfare' (ISEW) against the United States' GNP per capita. This confirmed the original finding that the two time-series had moved closely in step until about 1966. Between that date and 1986, however, the ISEW had remained roughly constant while US national income per head increased by 50 per cent, and more recently still, although GNP growth has continued, the ISEW has steadily declined.

Other workers have shown that a similar economic sea change has taken place in other countries. In Britain, for example, Tim Jackson and Nic Marks showed that between 1950 and 1974, the ISEW grew at much the same rate as GNP per head, but has declined so rapidly since then that by 1990 it was only 3 per cent greater than the 1950 level, despite national income per person having more than doubled over the forty-year period. In Germany, Hans Diefenbacher found that much the same had happened there except that the decline began later, in 1981, and has been very much more rapid – 40 per cent in just seven years (see figure 3). In other words, the economic systems of three of the leading industrial nations are now running backwards and achieving economic growth at the expense of their peoples' long-term economic welfare. The same thing could also be happening in Ireland.

GNP is not just a measure of benefits but of costs as well and the reason a country's GNP is no longer a proxy for its citizens' economic welfare is that the increasingly complex and indirect systems of production and distribution that a modern economy employs are increasing the costs more rapidly than the benefits by consuming a rising proportion of their output themselves. This is Fatima economics, so-called after an elderly arthritic Anglo-Nubian goat, whose West of Ireland keeper milked her and then fed her the milk back in an attempt to build her up.

Many components of the GNP total do little or nothing to improve personal well-being. For example, the proportion of national output

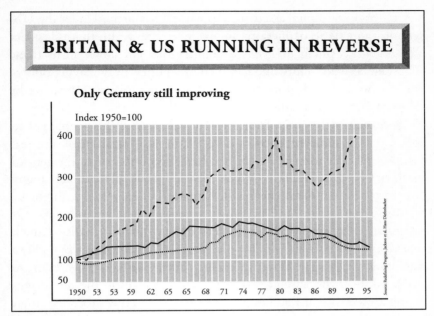

BRITAIN & US RUNNING IN REVERSE

Only Germany still improving

Index 1950=100

Figure 3

ploughed back into building new factories, roads and shopping centres is not available for people to spend on life's essentials and enjoyment. Nor is money for research, training, marketing, advertising, PR, transport, packaging, corporate legal and financial services, all activities that have been expanding more rapidly than the economy itself and thus reducing the amount available for popular consumption.

Bigger and bigger corrections ought to be made to the raw GNP figure to eliminate these distortions but, in Ireland as elsewhere, government statisticians largely fail to do so to avoid departing from the UN System of National Accounts and thus destroying international comparability. This is why Ireland's GNP statistics are still grossly inflated by the artificial pricing structures adopted by multinational companies based here to avoid overseas taxation. Just two companies, Pepsi-Cola and Coca-Cola, apparently contributed £600 million to the national income in a recent year although they had only 400 employees between them.

This is a particularly Irish problem. Every country, however, needs to correct its accounts to allow for income flows that arise from the consumption of capital assets such as natural resources. Under the UN system, though, no deductions are made for the wealth that is lost. As *The Economist* put it in 1989, 'a country that cut down all its trees, sold them as wood-chips and gambled the money away playing tiddly-winks would appear from its national accounts to have got richer in terms of GNP per person.'

And even if the proportion of national income the people get to spend stays a constant fraction of GNP so that, on average, the real value of the cash going through their bank accounts grows, the general level of people's welfare might not improve. There are many circumstances in which this could happen. For example, it might be because wealth may have become concentrated in fewer hands. Or because the growth process has increased the volume of traffic so much that people have to buy double-glazing to be able to sleep at night, a purchase which, far from increasing their welfare, fails even to maintain it. Or because growth has caused changes in the way things are organised so that families have to run a car to buy groceries rather than having them delivered as their parents once did, with the result that the part of their extra income that motoring costs consume is of no benefit to them. Growth changes the way the world works to such an extent that just because people have more money does not guarantee that they will be better off.

Jackson and Marks corrected for as many of the changes produced by growth as possible when they prepared their ISEW. For example, they adjusted each year's consumer expenditure figures for changes in the equality of income distribution on the basis that an extra £1000 was likely to be of much more benefit to someone on a low income than to someone who was very well off. They also allowed for changes over time in the amount of housework and other goods and services that people produced for themselves. Next they corrected for the increasing value of the services provided by the washing machines, televisions and any other consumer durables people owned. Another adjustment covered the benefits people received from the educational and health expenditures paid for by the State.

The subtotal they arrived at proved to be closely related to that year's per capita Gross National Product. Then they made corrections for such things as the cost of commuting, traffic accidents, water, air and noise pollution, the loss of farmland, the depletion of non-renewable resources, and long-term environmental damage, including that to the ozone layer. Up to 1974, these deductions grew roughly at the same rate as consumer expenditure, but since then they have grown much more rapidly, with the result that their index fell, indicating that the British people were on balance worse off.

So, once we've accepted that the annual growth figure is largely of interest to the business community and a very poor guide to anything for anyone else, perhaps we ought to calculate an annual ISEW figure for Ireland to see whether the quest for growth is making this country less sustainable, as it is almost everywhere else. Work on such an index is, in fact, going on at present, and Feasta, the newly formed Foundation for the Economics of Sustainability, hopes to publish it in May next year.

The third step is to work out just what it is about our economic system that causes it to crash into a depression if a minimum rate of growth is not achieved. I've recently done some work in this area and the results have been published under the title *The Ecology of Money*.[14] I haven't time to go into the details here but I think that one of the culprits is the fact that most – around 97 per cent – of our money gets into circulation because someone has gone into debt. This means that interest has to be paid on almost all the money we use and, to the extent that the banks make a profit out of those interest charges, they are constantly removing money from the circular flow. This would cause the economy to contract unless enough people were prepared to take on additional debts to borrow it back into circulation again. In other words, the money system we're using requires the total amount of debt to increase each year, but people won't be prepared to take on the extra debt to permit this unless the economy expands. So the answer to this problem is not to allow the commercial banks to create almost all of our money for us, but for the government to spend it into circulation. In Britain, it has been estimated[15] that such a change would enable taxes to be cut by 16 per cent. The change would also make our economic system much more stable.

The fourth step is to realise that the resources we are using to generate growth each year could be used in other ways. Generating growth just to keep people employed is about as sensible as having people dig holes and fill them in again if the growth doesn't bring any benefits. Indeed, if growth is actually making things worse, as it certainly seems to be socially and environmentally at present, it would be better to dig the holes. In other words, we could use the resources we're devoting to growth to cure poverty more directly – if we chose.

But do we have the choice? Thanks to globalisation, governments are required to run their countries in very specific ways because, if they don't, international investors will cause a financial crisis by shifting their funds elsewhere. As a result, I don't think it is possible to move to a stable, sustainable – and that means zero growth – world within the system we have constructed on the basis that economic growth of any sort that the market generated was the greatest good. And, if that's the case, Ireland has to seek to extract itself from all the international agreements that commit it to free trade and the free movement of capital so that it can regain its economic independence.

Other countries should do the equivalent too, of course, and I'm sure they will want to do so. Indeed, before too long, a global crisis will force governments to stop trying to generate growth continually just to please investors and to stay out of depressions. Instead, they will seek to change their economic systems from top to bottom. Our task then must be to have a major influence on the ways they do so.

NOTES

1. Pluto Press, London.
2. Central Bank of Ireland, *Bulletin* (Spring 1999), p. 57.
3. *The Earnings Distribution and Returns to Education in Ireland, 1987-94.* Another ESRI report, *Poverty in the 1990s,* shows that the percentage of persons receiving below half the average income rose from just over 15 per cent in 1973 to 21 per cent in 1994.
4. George A. Kaplan and others, 'Inequality in income and mortality in the United States: analysis of mortality and potential pathways', *British Medical Journal,* vol. 312 (20 April 1996), pp. 999-1003.
5. *Perinatal Statistics,* 1993, Department of Health, Government Publications Office, 1997.
6. Reported in *The Irish Times,* 25 September 1998.

7. Central Bank of Ireland, *Monthly Statistics*, No. 9 (1999).
8. Central Bank of Ireland, *Bulletin* (Spring 1999), p. 19.
9. Prepared mid-October, 1999.
10. Crispin Aubrey, 'Taming the Irish Tiger', *New Energy*, No. 2 (May 1999).
11. Patrick Smyth, 'Greenhouse gas emission strategy not going according to plan', *The Irish Times*, 21 May 1999.
12. No. 634, 21 January 1999.
13. Reported by Tim Radford in *The Guardian*, 15 April 1999.
14. Schumacher Society, Bristol, October 1999.
15. J. Robertson, *Monetary Policy and Fiscal Policy: The Question of Credit Creation* (circulated privately, August 1999).

7

IS BALANCE A MYTH?
CREATIVITY AWAKENS ONLY AT THE EDGE

JOHN O'DONOHUE

The Concept of Balance in a Theory of Creation

One of my favourite sentences in the Western philosophical tradition is from Leibnitz; it was subsequently used by Shelling and Heidegger: 'The real mystery is not that things are the way they are, but that there is *something* rather than nothing'. I think this is a great sentence, because it alerts one immediately to the mystery of the presence of things, which we so often tend to forget. In post-modern culture, we live increasingly in a virtual world and seem to have lost visceral and vital contact with the actual world.

Another way of looking at this statement is: the real mystery is that there is so much. Everywhere the human eye looks, everywhere the human mind turns, there is a huge panorama of diversity; the difference that lives in everything and between everything, the fact that no two stones, no two fields, no two faces or no two biographies are the same. The range and intensity of this difference is quite staggering. This is not an abstract thing. People who live in small farms in country areas could spend hours telling you about all the differences they experience between two places in the same field. Patrick Kavanagh spoke of 'the undying difference in the corner of a field'.

The difference that inhabits experience and the world is not raw chaos; it has a certain structure. It is quite amazing to consider the hidden, implicit structures that exist in all the natural things. For instance, the way water falls so elegantly, always with structure. Even the water from the tyres of a car as it goes through a motorway or street can have a beautiful structure. There is huge differentiation in the world, and its structure often seems to be one of duality; in other words, two sides of the one object or reality.

If you reflect on your own experience, you will see that you are already familiar with duality. There is light and darkness, beginning and ending, inside and outside, above and below, masculine and feminine, divine and human, time and eternity, soul and sense, word and silence. The really fascinating thing is not that these dualities are there, but the threshold where they actually meet each other. I believe that any notion of balance that is really authentic has to work with the notion of threshold. Otherwise, balance is just a functional strategy without any ontological depth or grounding. In the Western tradition, that line, that threshold between light and darkness, between soul and body, god and human, between ourselves and nature, has often become atrophied. When the threshold freezes, the two sides get cut off from each other and the result is dualism. That kind of separation has really blighted and damaged the Western tradition. You can see this in very simple ways. For instance, in Catholic Ireland there was a division between the soul and the senses. The senses were supposed to be bad, and the body pulled you down, whereas the soul wanted to bring you up. That split caused untold guilt and pain for people.

Duality, then, is informed by the oppositions that meet at this threshold. I would argue that an authentic life is a life that is aware of and willing to engage its own oppositions, and honourably inhabits that threshold where the light and darkness, the masculine and feminine and all the beginnings and endings of one's life engage. Sometimes, people who are very vociferous and moralistic are people who have erased the tug of opposition from their lives. They have little sense of the otherness that suffuses and surrounds them. Thus, they can allow themselves all kinds of moral platitudes and even moral judgements of others. It is lonely sometimes to hear them talk because, in their certainty, you can hear the hollow echo of a life only half-lived.

All creativity comes out of that spark of opposition where two different things meet. It is where each of us was conceived. Masculine and masculine, feminine and feminine on their own cannot procreate. It is the two sides, the two sister oppositions that create the unity. It is the same rhythm within subjectivity: there is a whole outer side to you, your name, face, role and identity, and then there is the hidden world you carry within you. I think that real balance is, in some sense, about action, where the living reality of your life balances what is within you with what you are meeting outside. One of the greatest duties of post-modern culture at the end of this millennium is to try to bring the personal and the communal, the individual and the universal together.

Experience is working all the time with duality, with that energy of opposition within you. You have no experience that does not have two sides to it. In a certain sense, all of your experience is a kind of narrative or story, with this deep underside that you never see, yet out of which all your possibilities come. Even though it is opaque, it constantly guides you and brings you places you never expected. That is the surprise and the unpredictability of life. In relation to the notion of balance, we have to begin to strive towards a concept of person or self that is sufficiently complex and substantial to do justice to our huge metaphysical needs at the end of this millennium.

One of the victims of media culture is the depth and interiority of the self. People are treated like images, like instances of general principles, but rarely are individuals taken and illuminated for their own unique depth. The history, narrative and possibilities they carry within themselves are usually sidelined in any description or presentation of them. It is frightening how our collusion with technology has damaged so much our sense of individuality and our sense of the secret and sacred world that every individual inhabits. This insidious reductionism is one of the most powerful forces of imbalance today.

Imagination
The imagination is the faculty that gives the duality within us expression and allows its forms of opposition to engage with each other. In the Western Christian tradition we gave a huge role to intellect and to will. The intellect was used to find out what the goal or object was and then the will drove it along the linear track towards it. This model of human sensibility brought us much beauty, but its neglect of the imagination has also cost us dearly. A human life can have everything – beauty, status, reputation, achievement, all kinds of possessions, but if the imagination is not awakened, all these lack presence and depth.

There are poor people who have absolutely nothing, but who have a depth of creative imagination that allows them, even in bleak circumstances, to inhabit a gracious, challenging and exciting world. The heart of it all is that there is an indissoluble, radical, subversive connection between mind and reality. The structures of your mind, the way your mind works, the way your consciousness moves, its patterns, actually determine the world you inhabit. You cannot separate the two of them. The awakened imagination brings us great riches. The imagination is not one-sided; it is passionately interested in wholesomeness and wholeness. The imagination is never tempted or attracted to the flat surface or to whatever is safe and perfect. Sometimes when you hear people talking about the human self you would think that it is made out of stainless steel and is meant to have this perfection and purity. But we are clay creatures, striving desperately towards the light.

The idea of the threshold is significant because the human body itself is actually a threshold. Each human individual is a threshold in many different ways. You are a threshold in that you are made out of clay. What keeps you alive is in the invisible air. Yet you belong neither to the earth out of which you have come, nor to the heavens towards which you strain. So, you are always in this oscillation, on this moving threshold. Within your own family you are also on a threshold – the threshold between all of the ancestral lines that meet in you, and the line that will go out from you. In many different ways the imagination tries to awaken, articulate and integrate all the presences that meet in us.

At the beginning of his book *The Phenomenology of Spirit*, Hegel says, '*Das wahre is das ganze*', i.e. the truth is whole. Most of the time when we are talking about things, we seem so sure that we are right, yet all we are giving are little minuscule, half-truth glimpses. To become wholesome, we need living connection with whole. Our access is always limited and partial; yet through the imagination, we can enter more elegantly into its field of creative tensions.

There are two great sentences in the Greek tradition: 'Know thyself' and 'Everything flows'. The human self is surrounded by change and is itself continually changing. Your body is constantly changing. In a philosophy class I once had, our professor told us that over a seven-year period all the cells in the body will have changed.

There was at the time someone in England who had been in prison for seven years and he appealed his sentence. His claim was that he was not the person now whom they had sentenced seven years before! So, there is this constant changing. In the West of Ireland, visually we are very aware of this, because the weather and the light changes all the time.

If everything was, as the Germans say, in *Stillstand,* or deadlocked in the same position, we would not need to worry about balance. We would all be totally fixated and atrophied in the one position. It is because there is so much movement and change that the notion of balance takes on such depth and urgency. The argument for change is put most memorably by Heraclitus, a philosopher in fifth-century Greece. He said that you can never step into the same river twice because if you step in at four o'clock and again at five past four, the river has completely changed, and you have changed as well. There is constant change all the time, and imagination is the most faithful force in helping change and continuity maintain a dialogue with each other.

Part of the reason we are so confused at the end of this millennium is that so much change has occurred, at such an acute and relentless pace, that we are not able to decipher and activate the lines of continuity into our own tradition. There is an intense isolation there, a haunting lonesomeness, especially in young people. They are uprooted and dislocated. Even adults a generation or two ahead of them are not able to speak their language. The isolation is intensified in that they are the relentless targets of marketing. Huge multinational marketing systems are targeting teenagers and what they are achieving is incredible. Parents or teachers could never get teenagers into uniforms and yet multinational corporations have done it. Teenagers are all wearing designer gear. The label is more important than the garment. At the most subversive times of their lives, they are indoctrinated with this peer virus. Again, it is money and greed that have turned teenagers into targets for commodities.

The imagination tries to take change and inhabit it in a way that allows it to be transfigurative rather than destructive. The lovely thing about the imagination is that, whereas the mind often sees change and thinks everything is lost, the imagination can always go deeper than the actual experience of the loss and find something else in it. There is an amazing difference between the way the mind sees something and the way the imagination sees something.

Imagination and the Balance with Otherness

Another lovely quality of the imagination is its passion for otherness. Otherness is a technical term, but it means, essentially, everything that is other than you. The easiest way to register the notion of otherness is to think of somebody you really dislike intensely. The experience of otherness registers most firmly in what we find strange or totally different from ourselves. One of the huge spiritual, psychological, philosophical and theological problems of post-modern culture is the question of otherness.

The world of media and corporate marketing has actually homogenised things completely and wants to make everything the same. The advertisement you see for Levi's over the Midtown Tunnel as you come into Manhattan is the same as the ad you'll see in Limerick or Dublin or even in the desert or the Middle East. There is an incredible difficulty for individual places and individual experiences to assert their own uniqueness and individuality. It is very difficult in mass culture to argue for a unique space – for what is individual and different. Yet one of the most important conversations in any life remains the conversation with what is other than you.

When people get into trouble psychologically, it is often because something comes upon them that frightens them, or paralyses them, so that they cannot move, work or function. It is something they would never have anticipated in themselves. This sudden confrontation with unexpected otherness becomes crippling. For instance, some people who are perfectionistic may find an otherness awakening in or around them that renders them helpless. One of the most threatening forms of otherness in any life is illness. It is a frightening thing that you can be going on with your life, thinking you have troubles, and then you run headlong into serious illness and your life and your world are absolutely altered.

The oppositions that are in us often constellate themselves in other ways, in terms of contradiction. It is interesting to see how the media handles contradiction. The media focuses on an image, but an image is always just one view of a thing, it is never the full view. If you want

the full view, you meet with a person face-to-face, or you read good
literature or listen to good music or look at a good painting or a good
landscape. Then the multi-dimensionality of a thing comes through.
The media is essentially like Plato's Cave – a parade of shadows that
we take for the real world. It is a huge subtraction from what is real.
To believe in the media as the actual vehicle of truth or the way to
'what truly is' can be very misleading. It is necessary to have the kind
of exploration that the media does, but on its own as sole authority, it
is totally insufficient. Its presentations grow ever more syncopated into
sound bites.

It is interesting that when the media notices a contradiction in
someone, the reportage turns merciless. Usually, it has to do with a fall
from a principle, because the media will inevitably have constructed
the image in the first place in such a way that a certain principle has
been embodied. When a contradiction emerges, there is a sensational
story. The media 'outs' people and, in certain instances where it has a
public interest dimension, this can be warranted. More often,
however, I believe it is a massive intrusion into the private lives of
individuals. While it may make a story today, the media light moves
quickly elsewhere, and the exposed individual is left with years of
struggle to put their life back together again.

What is interesting about contradictions is that each person is a
bundle of contradictions. Normally we are not aware of our
contradictory nature because there is so much of ourselves that we
keep completely hidden. Perhaps one of the reasons we are on this
planet is to try to become acquainted with all that is in us. When you
meet someone who is not afraid of themselves it is a lovely experience.
They might be a mass of contradictions but at least they have patience
with their own otherness. I think that, in many ways, the images of self
that we see reflected in political life, religious life and media life are
totally inadequate to carry the depth that is in us.

In a contradiction, the two sides are meeting. An opposition is
happening; it has come alive with great tension and energy. It can be
a frightening time in a person's life, but also a very interesting time.
Usually, the way we settle and compromise with ourselves is by
choosing one side over the other side, and we settle for that
reductionism until something awakens the other side, and then the

two of them are engaged. I was talking to somebody who was going through a huge conflict trying to decide if he should do A or if he should do B. A wise friend of his said to him, 'If it's either/or, it's neither.' The idea is that at the heart of the opposition there is something else coming through. That is where I think the notion of balance is really very powerful, because balance is a providential thing that allows something new to emerge from the depths of crisis and contradiction. This suggests faith in a third force that often endeavours to emerge through the oppositions that are coming alive in us.

The Myth of Balance

I want to explore the *myth* of balance. I am using the word 'myth' in two senses. Firstly, in its colloquial sense, the sense that myth is something that is not factually true – it is fantasy. Secondly, in its more profound sense, which is the idea of the mythical. The great myths are universal stories about dimensions of the gods, of ourselves and of nature. Usually they are stories in which the origin of a thing can be perceived. They are stories of what cannot actually be told. A myth is a narrative. For instance, you have the myth of Genesis, with Adam and Eve in the garden, or the story of Odysseus who got lost and was on his way home for thirty years. Myths and fairytales are profound communicators of wisdom in very subtle ways. All the folk cultures, even the most ancient ones, always had stories about the way everything began, and these stories in some way were the first attempts to balance people's precarious presence in a strange world. This ties in with the notion of cosmos, which is the idea of order. The *Oxford English Dictionary* includes these two aspects in its definition of 'balance'. Firstly, balance is 'an apparatus for weighing consisting of a beam poised so as to move freely on a central pivot with a scale pan at each end', or secondly, balance is 'the stability due to the equilibrium of forces within a system'.

I believe that balance also includes passion, movement, rhythm, urgency and harmony. Balance is not a dead notion. Balance as a monolithic thing would not be balance at all; it would be total imbalance, because there is something in balance that, in order to be what it is, requires the loyal weight of the opposite and opposing force.

When you talk about balance, you are talking about the discovery or the unveiling of things, of a secret rhythm of order. I believe that balance can never be merely subjective or monological.

I want to sketch briefly in philosophical terms a cognitive theory of balance. Most theories of balance are non-cognitive and inevitably end up as either strategies or platitudes. There are two main ways of looking at balance – the conservative and the liberal views, or the empiricist and the idealist views. The first one is that balance is a strategy. You hear people saying that you must have balance in your life. If you do not have balance, everything will turn chaotic. Balance, then, is an external frame imposed on experience from the outside. It controls things and keeps the chaos away.

Such strategies of balance are often no more than veiled repression. For instance, you may feel a deep complexity of feeling, but you pretend that you do not feel. You bury everything in the basement of your mind. Jung used to call this 'the return of the repressed'. No sooner have you expelled something that you cannot accept about yourself out the front door than it has made its way in the back door and is waiting there to confront you again. It is a strange thing about consciousness that if you try deliberately to get rid of something or to stop thinking about something, you only end up reinforcing it.

This idea finds humorous expression in a story I heard somewhere. A man went to see a guru as he was finding it difficult to meditate because his mind was scattered. The guru said to him, 'I want you to go home and *not* think about monkeys.' Surprised at the advice, because monkeys never figured in his mind, the man nevertheless returned home intending to carry out the advice. When he came back, he started to try not to think about monkeys. First there was one monkey and then there were two monkeys, then there were ten monkeys. Within two hours he was back to the guru as his mind had become an exclusive monkey jungle. Thus, there is a strange thing in consciousness, in the mind, that if you make an issue of something it can expand and possess you. This seems to be what happens with bitterness. A bitter person cannot decide to be bitter between 7.00 and 7.30 on Saturday evenings, because if you are bitter, it is within you everywhere. Resentment is exactly the same kind of thing. Resentment, bitterness, defeat, despair, even depression – all of these share this pervasive quality. When I sit in front of somebody who is clinically, chronically depressed, the feeling that I have sometimes is that the person is not actually there. The fascinating question is, where are they? So repression is often the outcome when balance is approached as a functional, imposed strategy.

Another dimension of balance as a functional strategy is fear. If you are afraid of things, you will stay in line; this often has to do with authority. On German television, in the last six or seven weeks, on the tenth anniversary of the fall of East Germany, they have been replaying old news excerpts. It is unbelievable viewing. Two days before the whole thing started, there was Hoeneker, leader of East Germany, with all the leaders of the Communist world, and they were all paying tribute to one another. Ceaucescu was in the middle of them. And the whole facade was within inches of collapsing, never to return. Flexibility is balance and balance is flexibility. When a thing hardens it cannot bend. It can only break. When a thing or system becomes totally atrophied, the smallest incision can cause the whole thing to vanish as if it were a false garment.

Another dimension of balance as a functional strategy, one that also keeps people in line, is the whole world of religious edict and theology. Many people in Ireland held their lives in a certain kind of balance because they were theologically terrified. We are coming out of that now. This theory of balance, which is a frame from outside, usually works with an unexamined belief in the given facts. It is very empiricist, it is one-dimensional and it is usually ideological. It is non-cognitive in the sense that it is never worked out nor its deeper grounding ever questioned. It is given, and because it is given, it is always in the service of some elite group or some vested interest that wants the balance to hold for some ideological reason.

The opposite view of balance is that balance is a purely subjective invention – I can invent, sustain and implement my own order. This, of course, is equally false. Literary tragedy, for instance, unmasks this as illusion. Tragedy presents great passionate individuals who attempt to establish their own order and their action brings them into total conflict with the hidden order, which uncoils on top of them, and completely changes the world they inhabit. Therefore, balance is neither a fixed empirical thing nor an invented, subjective thing.

Rather, balance is an implicit equilibrium that emerges in the fair-play of opposing forces – opposing sister forces.

Balance yields itself in the dialogue and dialectic of passionate forces. It is not monological. Much of what passes for conversation in post-modern culture is merely intercepting monologues. If you watch television discussion programmes or listen to the radio, you hear little true conversation. When you yourself are involved in a really genuine conversation with another person, you will remember it for weeks because something unexpected shifts or happens in the dynamic of conversation. It is no accident that at the infancy of Western culture, we have the great models of conversation in Plato's dialogues. In true dialogue something truly other and unexpected emerges. What I am talking about here is a theory of growth; not economic growth, but the growth of life and experience that works in this shifting balance between dialogue on the one hand and dialectic on the other hand.

It is interesting to consider balance in terms of the physical human body, in terms of anatomy. The French phenomenologist Merleau-Ponty has wonderful things to say about the human body. The body is not an object to think about. Rather, it is a grouping of lived-through meanings, which move towards equilibrium. Your body is not just an object, it is actually all the meanings that people have towards your body. It is moving towards equilibrium.[1] The place where your balance is regulated is also the place where your hearing and listening are activated. This is in the fluid of the semi-circular canals of the inner ear. The eighth nerve goes through this liquid in the inner ear. It gives the impulses to the brain and tells the brain literally where you are.[2] For instance, in cases of vertigo, where there is irritation or some damage, you have the feeling that the room has actually moved, but of course it has not. People also have that experience 'the morning after the night before', when you suddenly think that the laws of causality have changed and that the room is shifting around.

Therefore, true balance in the body is linked to listening, but also metaphorically, true balance is linked to an attentiveness that allows you to engage fully with a situation, a person or your culture or memory so that the hidden balance within can emerge. Listening can actually be a force that elicits the balance and allows it to emerge. Balance is not subjective. Neither is balance to be simply achieved or reached by human beings. True balance is a grace. It is something that is given to you. When you watch somebody walking the high wire, you know that they could tumble any second. That is the way we all are. Though we prefer to forget and repress it, we live every moment in the condition of contingency. There are people who got up this morning, prepared for another normal day, but something happened, some event, news, disappointment or something wonderful, and their lives will never be the same again after this day in the world. This is a day they will never forget. Very often our actual balance in the world as we go is totally precarious, without our realising it. Balance invites us not to take ourselves too seriously.

I spent five years in Germany and I loved German culture, music, thinking and philosophy. But the Germans would not be known as post-graduates in the whole area of humour or spontaneity! There is in the Irish psyche, I think, a kind of flexibility and a grounding humour that actually levels things and balances things out. I have talked to people who worked with Irish people in all kinds of areas in the Third World where there was poverty and war. They often said that the Irish brought a certain humour into the situation that allowed others to forget for a while the awfulness that was around them. This, of course, is a direct derivative of our history. We have had a history of incredible pain, misery, poverty and suffering in this country, which is often forgotten now. In these politically correct and tiger economic times, it is embarrassing to remember what has happened to us. The truth is that terrible things happened to us. And the only way we were able to come through it was to win some distance from it. Often, Irish humour has this subtext of knowing the complete horror, but yet deciding not to bend to its ravages. That is why Beckett is a sublime Irish writer, because he can bring the blackness and the humour to such incredible balance and harmony.

Balance can be beautifully achieved in the human body, especially in dance. I remember one night in Lisdoonvarna, watching, in a small little corner of the pub, about thirty-five human bodies starting to dance. There was a band playing and I saw these people in the corner and I thought to myself that they could never dance in such a small space. Yet, when the music started and brought rhythm, they were wheeling in and out and nobody crashed into anyone else. So sometimes when another rhythm is present, balance becomes possible in the most unpredictable situations.

Balance and the Millennium

In the concluding section, I want to reflect on balance at the millennium threshold. A millennium threshold is said to be a time of imbalance and disturbance. To be honest, I believe that much of the excitement about the millennium is a result of manipulation. For a few cultures, this is not the millennium. If you could talk to stones and rivers and oceans or even sheep, they would be asking why these humans are getting worked up about the millennium. The earth and the ocean and the rain and the wind and the trees and the cows and the calves have no idea that we are entering a new millennium. But, because we are all fixated on the millennium, there is a lot happening and it is a huge threshold; and in a way we are coming into it vulnerable and very exposed.

There are several agents of imbalance. One is the whole consumerist trend of post-modern culture. In philosophical terms, what is going on here is a reduction of the 'who' question about presence and person, to the 'what' question and the 'how' question. It's an obsession, almost a regression to what Freud called the 'oral stage'. The key tenet here is that consumption creates identity. I was over in Atlanta, Georgia, on a book tour early on in the year. I saw a weed there called the *kutsu;* it grows a foot in a day. This weed is set to take over and if it's not cut back it will take over completely. It struck me as a profound image for consumerism. Most of us are moving through such an undergrowth of excess that we cannot sense the shape of ourselves anymore. Sometimes you meet a writer who gives you a little instrumentation to make a clearance here. For me, such a writer is William Stafford, the wonderful American poet. In the latest book from his estate on the nature of poetry, *Crossing Unmarked Snow,* here are four sentences:

> The things you do not have to say make you rich.
> Saying the things you do not have to say weakens your talk.
> Hearing the things you do not need to hear dulls your hearing.
> The things you know before you hear them, those are you and this is the reason that you are in the world.

There is a massive functionalism at the heart of our times, a huge imbalance in post-modernity, primarily because certain key conversations are not taking place. One conversation that is not taking place is a conversation between the privileged and the poor. We are an immensely privileged minority. We think the Western world is the whole world. Yet, in fact, we are just a tiny minority. The majority of the world is living in the most awful circumstances. A friend of mine in London who has done research on this told me that 80 per cent of the people in the world have never used a telephone. It is a sobering statistic. Corally disturbing is the fact that we are here now in a comfortable setting talking about things we love. At the moment, there is a woman, a young mother, going through a dustbin in some barrio in South America for the tenth time today, for crumbs for her starving children whom she loves just as much as we love our children. The disturbing question is why is that person out there carrying that and why can we be here in comfort? I do not know the answer, but I do know that we are privileged, and that the duty of privilege is absolute integrity. That is a huge part of balance, the question of integrity and integration. Without integrity, there can be no true integration.

Another conversation that is not happening, which is a terrifying non-event, is the conversation between the Western culture and Islam. Certain people are making attempts to do it, such as Edward Saied, the NPR reporter, the American novelist Jacki Lyden, the theologian Michael Sells, and Prince Charles. Yet it is a conversation that is not happening essentially at a cultural level. We have a caricature of what Islam is. They have the same caricature of us. In caricature and false imagery and projection, so much violence, destruction and wars are already seeded. It is bleakly ironic in a culture that is obsessed with communication technology that the actual art and vital content of communication is shrinking all the time.

In relation to the Irish context, there is an urgent need for greater dialogue between the forces of city culture and the rural domain. The city has become the power centre in Western culture. It is where the most significant powers of media, finance, politics and religion are located. Naturally, then, the media, in reflecting these activities, inevitably does so through an urban filter of language, thought and style. Were one to watch television every night for a week to see what images from rural life emerge on television, one would find few real references to the life on the land. Also the public language describing rural life is a language determined by the city and it is usually not an understanding language. People who live in the country know that you have to live in the country to know what the country is actually like. The country is not so much a community, it is a network. It has deep intricate thickets of connection that cannot be seen from outside. Folk-life has depth and shadow that the media never comes near. The language used by the media about the country often reveals its distance from the cut and thrust of the rural sensibility. Even the word rural is diminutive, as in 'He's a very rural type'. The word 'peasant' is also diminutive. If one looks around for words about farming, to show the beauty and profound dignity of what it is, it is difficult to find any words in the public forum. I think farming is one of the great life callings. It has become very difficult now, but it is a great artistic, creative calling.

To Find Balance in an Ireland of Inner Turbulence

At the threshold to the millennium, Ireland is in some turbulence. Many of the sacred facades have been pulled down in the domains of religion, politics and finance. The unmasking has revealed corruption in all of these domains. These revelations have dulled and damaged our sense of and belief in ideals. They have caused disillusionment and cynicism. The positive side of this is that it relieves us of over-dependence on false crutches; it invites us to depend more on our own courage and critique. But, there is a danger in all of this clearing out that we will throw out many of the values that have sustained, refined and deepened us as a people. I do believe that Ireland has something very special, something very unique in Europe, and we really are at a crossroads with it. Of course, not everything was perfect. With the old kind of lifestyle, there was a lot of poverty, drudgery and slavery of work. There were the valleys of the squinting windows. There was the awful repression of the thirties and forties in Ireland, when so many lovely innocent people were totally sinned against in the most sinister ways. There is that negative shadow in our tradition. But this is not the full story. Our tradition also has huge spiritual, imaginative and wisdom riches. There was a sense of proportion, a sense of belonging, a sense of being in a tradition that we are now in danger of losing completely.

Ireland is predominantly a folk culture. The issue for me at the level of principle is that it seems to take hundreds of years for a folk culture to weave itself, and yet so often, with the infusion of the consumerism virus, such a cultural fabric unravels in a very short time. The question then is: what hidden resources are there within our culture that can help us to stand at this very severing crossroads and still hold what is precious to us from our tradition, to guide us over the threshold into the new millennium? It is a very important question because many people who are spiritually, theologically and philosophically awakened look to Ireland and see something here that we ourselves often do not see. It will demand great vision and leadership to engage all the tensions of our present turbulence and find a path that still vitally connects with the heart of the Irish tradition and yet engages the modern milieu openly and creatively. A tradition is a living presence. To reacquaint ourselves with the brightness as well as the darkness in our tradition could be an important first step.

The pace and rate of development in contemporary Ireland is quite alarming. Ireland seems to be a huge target for major development. There are people who would sell everything for any kind of development and short-term gain. This is difficult to comprehend, given the terrible history we have had of being exiled from our own land. Now that we have finally got the land, it is almost as if we are not able to be at ease with it and inhabit it and recognise its beauty. I am not saying that there should be no development, of course there should be. People need to live. I am saying that we should have greater openness towards forms of development that do not destroy our environment. It is hugely important because it is not just ours – we are custodians of it for our children, who will inhabit it after us.

A government is elected constitutionally to protect a people against conquest, yet the economic consumerist conquest that is going on in Ireland is just unbelievable. In Connemara, the people say *'Tá an nádúr ag imeacht as na daoine'*, i.e. the nature is going out of people. When people have very little, it is natural for them to be close. I am not romanticising poverty; it is a horrible thing, full of drudgery. Think of all the people who had to emigrate because there was nothing for them. But yet there was some kind of *nádúr* or closeness. It seems to be impossible for a culture to develop economically and get really rich and yet maintain the same *nádúr* and closeness. So the question is: where could we find new places to awaken something in us in order that we do not lose that sense of *nádúr* and of belonging with each other?

Our heritage, rather than being something that can enable us to stand critically, worthily and courageously on the threshold of this new millennium, is now being converted into almost a fastfood product, that can be read off in ten minutes by a visiting tour bus somewhere. This is a very important issue. There's an ancient memory and a tradition that has huge archaic layers. We should be a lot more confident and a lot more courageous as we go into the new millennium and we should try to work with an idea of balance that is equal to that complex history and that somehow allows us to stand with a critical kind of sense at the edge of this new millennium and cross over with a certain kind of confidence. I just want to finish off by quoting the last paragraph from my book *Eternal Echoes: Exploring Our Hunger to Belong;* it summarises the tension of balance in desire as it navigates between longing and belonging.

> In the pulse beat is the life and the longing, all embraced in the great circle of belonging, reaching everywhere, leaving nothing and no one out. This embrace is mostly concealed from us who climb the relentless and vanishing escalator of time and journey outside where space is lonesome with distance. All we hear are whispers, all we see are glimpses; but each of us has the divinity of imagination which warms our hearts with the beauty and depth of a world woven from glimpses and whispers, an eternal world that meets the gaze of our eyes and the echo of our voices to assure us that from all eternity we have belonged and to answer the question that echoes at the heart of all longing: while we are here, where is it that we are absent from?

NOTES

1. I am indebted to Dr Lelia Doolan, a passionate student of Merleau-Ponty, for this reference.
2. Dr John Winters of Moycullen explained this anatomical perspective to me.

A VIEW FROM THE CHAIR

MARIAN HARKIN

My instinct told me that all parts of this process were important –
pausing for reflection, listening, assimilation of the message and
audience participation. These were all an integral part of the whole
experience. So it wasn't a case of 'flying by the seat of your pants'. I felt
a real sense of responsibility, just like the conductor in an orchestra
who has no role in the playing of the instruments but who must ensure
harmony in the performance.

One thing I admire about Richard Douthwaite is that he disturbs
your comfort zone. Just when you thought that economically we were
getting it together in Ireland, he shattered some of the basic
assumptions about economic growth. He questioned the idea of
economic growth as an indicator of progress and suggested that as a
nation we should aim for sustainability, not growth.

In our rush to maximise growth we have been forced to overlook
other indicators of success and failure in our society. According to
Richard, growth benefits individuals and corporations, not society as
a whole. It has contributed to increased stress, housing problems,
damage to the environment and a widening gap between the 'haves'
and the 'have-nots'.

What disturbed my comfort zone was his analysis of the political
reality, the fact that we must carry on with the process of growth,
otherwise we face a crisis that no government could survive. He
suggested that we are on a treadmill going round and round; if we
don't grow we will lose our international competitiveness, and yet the
growth we persue will benefit few, impoverish many and endanger the
planet. I had this impression of us all chasing our tails, running just to
stand still. He didn't quite scare me out of my wits as he promised, but
I shifted in my seat a few times.

Before John O'Donohue arrived there was an air of expectancy in
the room. I was one of the people there who had not heard him speak

before, and while I had dipped into his book *Anam Cara* – and I might add I was mightily impressed – I still wondered about this person who could generate such anticipation.

He was soft-spoken, yet held his audience in the palm of his hand. There was a stillness in the room that I believe was entirely generated by his manner of speaking, and by his exploration of what is above, beyond, yet within each one of us. Reading that last sentence again, I'm not sure that it will make a great deal of sense to people who were not at the conference, but that was my impression on the day.

LIST OF CONTRIBUTORS

Harry Bohan: Fr Harry Bohan is the director of Rural Resource Development Ltd and the Founder of Rural Housing Organisation/ Rural Resource Organisation. He is involved in a number of family/ community initiatives including Cahercalla Hospital/Hospice. He has written several books and articles on the theme of the Christian view of economic development. He completed his post-graduate studies at the University of Wales. His MSc thesis was 'The Growth of Cities in Britain'.

Tom Collins: Dr Tom Collins is the director of the Centre for Adult and Community Education in the National University of Ireland, Maynooth. Maynooth is now the major third-level provider of adult education in Ireland and has been a major contributor to the professionalisation of adult and community education and to its application in a wide array of locally based development initiatives. Dr Collins has been active in promoting innovative responses to the educational needs of the most disadvantaged sectors of Irish society. He has played a leading role in conducting research in this field and in initiating educational programmes to counter disadvantage. He was a key contributor to the recent Green Paper on 'Adult Education in An Era of Lifelong Learning', produced by the Department of Education and Science.

Stephen R. Covey: Recognised as one of *Time Magazine's* twenty-five most influential people, Dr Stephen Covey is co-founder and vice-chairman of Franklin Covey Company, the largest management and leadership development organisation in the world. To date he has travelled to twenty-seven countries teaching whole-life leadership and effective time management. Covey's newest book, *Living the 7 Habits: Stories of Courage and Inspiration,* illustrates real-life stories from people and organisations who have been successfully affected by the principles embodied in his international best-selling business book,

The 7 Habits of Highly Effective People, which has been translated into 32 languages and has sold more than 12 million copies in 75 countries throughout the world. Dr Covey is the recipient of the Thomas More College Medallion for continuing service to humanity and has been awarded four honorary doctorate degrees.

John Cushnahan: John Cushnahan is a member of the European Parliament. He is currently vice president of the Foreign Affairs Committee. He is a graduate in Education from Queens University, Belfast, a member of the Institute of Public Relations, former general secretary, chief whip, and leader of the Alliance Party. The collapse of the last Northern Ireland Assembly in 1986 brought a premature end to his political career in Northern Ireland. Despite having no seat and no income, he remained leader of the Alliance Party until September 1987, when he resigned as Alliance Party leader. He was invited by Fine Gael to contest the European Elections in 1989, and was elected. During the 1989-94 term of the European Parliament, he was vice president of the Regional Affairs Committee, and a member of the Social and Agricultural Committees.

Richard Douthwaite: Richard Douthwaite worked as economic adviser to the government of the West Indian island of Montserrat in the early 1970s and, after a period running his own business, as a journalist specialising in economic and environmental topics. His book *The Growth Illusion: How Economic Growth Enriched the Few, Impoverished the Many and Endangered the Planet* appeared in 1992 and will be reissued in an extensively updated form this autumn. He has also written *Short Circuit* (1996), which explores the ways in which communities around the world are becoming more self-reliant. Since 1974 he has lived with his wife and family outside Westport, County Mayo, in a house they built for themselves.

Marian Harkin: Marian Harkin is a secondary school teacher at the Mercy College, Sligo. She has been a community activist in the voluntary sector for the past thirteen years. Living in Manorhamilton, she was elected as Leitrim representative onto the Council for the West in 1994. She became chairperson in 1996 and led the campaign to retain Objective 1 Status for Connacht/Ulster. She has already been appointed to the Government Task Force on Western Development. In 1998 she was elected chairperson of the Thirteen-County Committee for the Retention of Objective 1 Status. She is a member of the National Statistics Board. She contested the recent European Elections as an independent candidate in Connacht/Ulster and polled remarkable well on her first venture into mainstream politics.

Kevin Kelly: Kevin Kelly is the author of the bestselling personal development book *How? When You Don't Know How* and the upcoming release *Inside Out . . . Back To A Life Less Limiting.* A passionate communicator, Kevin is a great believer in jumping in at the deep end. In the past he has lived and worked with the Indians in Peru, met with remarkable masters in Nepal, India and Tibet, in addition to training and speaking in America, Australia, Germany, Holland and Ireland. His company, Kevin Kelly Unlimited, is dedicated to exhaustively researching the area of personal potential or, more specifically, highlighting the path to personal happiness.

Ciaran Lynch: Ciaran Lynch is the director of Rural Development in the Tipperary Rural and Business Development Institute and was the Senior Executive Planner with Clare County Council for thirteen years. He is a Town Planner, with degrees in Social Science and Social Planning and diplomas in Town Planning and Administrative Science. He is also a member of the Irish Planning Insitute and has nearly twenty-five years experience in planning and community development. During his time with Clare County Council he was involved in a wide range of community development initiatives. He is particularly interested in developing mechanisms for participation by local people in the management of their own areas and for the development of partnership between the public agencies, private enterprise and communities.

Catherine McGeachy: Catherine McGeachy is Managing Director of Vision Consultants, a company focused on effecting value change in individuals and organisations. A charismatic communicator, in the past twenty years she has worked with many micro-chip companies both in Ireland and Great Britain on the areas of communications, personal development, teamwork, customer care, time management and empowerment. Prior to this she was Counsellor for the Open University's Open Business School for five years and a tutor on its management and personal selection programmes. Between 1979 and 1991 she lectured on information systems and human communications in the University of Limerick.

Miriam Moore: Dr Miriam Moore is a clinical psychologist whose passion in life is the study of spiritual beings having human experiences. Her professional work over the past twenty-five years includes research, corporate training courses, individual coaching for business executives and regular contributions to various publications. She runs a private psychotherapy practice and is a consultant to the EU on mental health projects. She holds an advanced practitioner's certificate from the EMDR Institute in California – EMDR is an accelerated form of psychotherapy for the treatment of stress and Post-traumatic Stress Disorder (PTSD). She produced the first report on PTSD for the UN peace-keeping veterans. She received her PhD in clinical psychology from Trinity College, Dublin.

John O'Donohue: John O'Donohue is a poet, philosopher and environmental activist who lives in Connemara, County Galway. He is a native of Fanore, Co Clare and as such has strong ties to the famous Burren region of North Clare. He is author of the international bestseller *Anam Cara: A Book of Celtic Wisdom,* which was described by the *Irish Times* as a 'phenomenon' to be read and re-read forever. He recently published *Eternal Echoes: Exploring Our Hunger To Belong.* He has also produced several audio cassettes under the general title *Wisdom From the Celtic World.* He was awarded a PhD in philosophical theology in Tubingen, Germay.

Fintan O'Toole: Fintan O'Toole is a columnist with *The Irish Times.* He was born in Dublin in 1958. He is married to Clare and they have two children. Since qualifying from University College, Dublin, he worked as a freelance journalist. He bacame the arts editor for *The Sunday Tribune,* editor of *Magill* magazine and has been a columnist with *The Irish Times* since 1988. He is also drama critic for *The New York Daily News*. He has published numerous books including *Meanwhile Back at the Ranch*, *Ex-Isle of Erin* and *A Traitor's Kiss: The Life of Richard Brinsley Sheridan*.

Dr Mary Redmond is a solicitor who runs her own practice specialising in Employment Law, and is on the Board of the Labour Relations Commission. She is founder of the Irish Hospice Foundation, of which she is now Patron. She is a Director of the Bank of Ireland Group and of Jefferson Smurfit Plc and has previously been a member of the Equality Employment Agency and of the Higher Education Authority. Since 1996 she has been Professor (Adjunct) at the National College of Industrial Relations and she is also a member of the Institute of Directors of Ireland and Fellow of the Royal Society of Arts. Prior to 1985 when she set up her own practice, she was involved in academic life at University College, Dublin and, before that, Churchill College. She is an honorary member of the Senior Common Room at Somerville College, Oxford. Her doctorate from Cambridge is on Termination of Employment. She has written several books on Employment Law and one on Constitutional Law. Her second edition of *Dismissal Law* is about to be published.

Redefining Roles and Relationships: Our Society in the New Millennium

Conference 2000

Conference '98 posed the question 'Are We Forgetting Something?' and dealt with the need to achieve a balance between a caring society and a consumer-oriented society in this era of the Celtic Tiger.

Conference '99, 'Working Towards Balance', continued the debate by trying to recognise the human dimension of the workplace in this increasingly career and work-oriented society.

Conference 2000 will bring this one step further into the personal realm by addressing the topic 'Redefining Roles and Relationships'.

Conference 2000

Conference Centre, West County Hotel,
Ennis, Co Clare
8-10 November 2000

For further information please contact:
Máire Johnston, Conference Co-ordinator
Rural Resource Development Ltd
Town Hall, Shannon, Co Clare
Tel 061 361 144 • Fax 061 361 954
Email rrd@eircom.net or millcon.ennis@eircom.net